Charas

CHARAS
The Improbable
Dome Builders

Syeus Mottel

The Song Cave &
Pioneer Works Press

This book is dedicated to everything that Is.

Acknowledgements

To David T. Paul for his vision, to Eva Galan for her sharp editorial eye, to Anthony Meisel for consistent advice, to David Karabell for watchfulness, to Connie Bessie for cogent observations, to John Palmer for masterful photographic assistance, to Elizabeth Mohr for being congenial, to Helen Wright and John Koch of Leitz, Inc., to Bucky for his inspiration, to Michael Ben-Eli for his friendship and finally to the young men and women of CHARAS who allowed me into their private moments.

Author's Note

The story in this book revolves around CHARAS—a community action group—and an event, a unique project that R. Buckminster Fuller and Michael Ben-Eli had developed with its members. For five months (September, 1972–January, 1973), on a nearly day by day process of obser-vation and encounter, I lived through the elation, drudgery, lassitude, conviviality, depression, exhaustive effort, humor, rage and eventual success of the young men and women of CHARAS. The process of discovery was equally vibrant for me.

In my other activities as a theatre/film director and photographer, I have usually been in a controlling position. It was highly revealing to be the reacter and recorder of an event, rather than the initiator or guide of an event. I observed the strengths and weaknesses of others and had to adapt my equilibrium to whatever was being pro-jected without overt judgment or comment. My function was to be there and absorb the situation without conscious selection.

There were moments of great exhil-aration as well as moments of ennui. The entire event was a lesson in interpersonal and group dynamics. It was testimonial to the extraordinary forces buried in all people but seldom tapped. I can only express my thanks to all who made this event possible and my participation viable. It was a totally absorbing and enriching adventure. I look forward to the next one.

—August, 1973

9

10

Contents

Preface to the New Edition

Prior to tracking down reproduction rights, and prior to the joys of uncovering supplemental archival material and the editorial decisions of what to do with it all, the republication process begins with two important questions. The first question is: does the work have value for a contemporary audience? If the answer is yes, the second question becomes: how do we as publishers navigate between that value and potential blind spots in the work both as an historical object and the way it frames issues of class, race, gender, and power? For this republication of *CHARAS: The Improbable Dome Builders,* by Syeus Mottel, the answers could be summed up in a line found on the back cover of the original edition: "It is important to remember in this instance that the process is more important than the product."

As a final product, this book is a fascinating account of six ex-gang members who came together around the project of building a geodesic dome in a vacant lot on the Lower East Side of Manhattan, and the ways they grappled with pressing issues of life in the United States during the Vietnam War Era: the urban housing crisis, rising poverty, increasing levels of violence, and the systematic oppression of immigrants, women, and people of color. Though much time has passed and new technologies and materials have emerged that are more advanced for such projects, the issues they faced remain. People continue to struggle for food, shelter, and recognition all over the world, and many are being priced out of neighborhoods across cities as the viral paths of gentrification seem to multiply faster than their communities can work to preserve themselves against it. Mottel's book still speaks to these issues because it is concerned with process over product. More than simply a documentation of the project, and more than the inspiring story of this group called CHARAS, it is the record of a kind of template for how people might come together by activating empty spaces *before* gentrification.

While the goal of the project was to develop the skills to be able to replicate the dome on land in upstate New York and escape life in the City, as it unfolded and the people of CHARAS observed the mark they were making on their community, they stayed and continued the work to improve and preserve that community. CHARAS has sustained and expanded its reach for years since, and is responsible for many of the community gardens, arts initiatives, after-school programs, and cultural centers of the Lower East Side. Today, more than four decades later, CHARAS continues to be an invaluable resource.

13

It is this process from notions of escape to empowering activism and engagement that Mottel captured and shared in *CHARAS: The Improbable Dome Builders,* which proves to be its enduring value and the reason for its republication. While no language of the original has been altered, this new edition has been redesigned, and certain typographical errors have been corrected. This edition also contains previously unpublished photographs discovered in storage by Syeus' son Matthew, and an interview with CHARAS' mentor on the Dome Building Project, Michael Ben-Eli, which contextualizes the project as an early example of how practical community involvement is more transformative than utopian ambitions. In reaching a new generation of readers, *CHARAS: The Improbable Dome Builders* will continue to challenge and inspire the ways we participate in and care for our global community. It still is after all, to lift a line from Bucky Fuller, "Everybody's Business."

—The Song Cave & Pioneer Works Press

Everybody's Business
R. Buckminster Fuller

Man born absolutely helpless and uninformed had to live through ages of ignorance and scarcity. Only a minute percentage became privileged minorities who physically overpowered other men and managed to live in relative abundance.

What we are coming into now is an extraordinary era in which all humanity is learning enough about productivity and nature's generalized principles to discover that not only can we take care of the few but also provide for all, taking care of the 99 percent of humanity who up to now were have-nots. And this is not a matter of one wise man or a few wise men providing for the ignorant 99 percent. It is a matter of the 99 percent becoming literate and knowing what it's all about.

All around the world, extraordinary communication systems are developing. This is a recent development, unique to our century, in which every human is becoming aware of everyone else, which makes the young realize that the old world has been going on outworn principles, and encourages the young to go forth spontaneously and intuitively to make mutually logical and desirable moves.

People who have been in the most abject poverty—who were the most "led," or who were the most illiterate, under influence of economic pressures, such as that of mechanization of farming—began to flow into the big cities and got really stranded and were victimized in a myriad of ways.

So we have in great cities like New York or Chicago or Los Angeles a fantastic amount of destitute humanity, with people greatly demoralized, trapped in the pattern of yesterday's ignorance.

There is nothing more exciting to me now than the fact that within the community on these streets I find leaders emerging who don't just want to take the law into their own hands, who don't just want to protest, but who, with a very deep and intuitive earnestness and dawning awareness, want to make things work.

To my amazement I found myself being called in to help gang leaders in Chicago, New York and Los Angeles. At first when I came to meet with them, my language scared them; they shied away. But then they came back again to develop projects with some of my young associates and students.

In particular, a group in New York, once part of the Real Great Society and now called CHARAS, could stand up in great calmness and equanimity and say, "We got heads on our shoulders, and we can employ them to work out something new and useful."

They had heard about my geodesic domes, and they thought maybe they'd like to get into the country, put up a few of these domes, and start living away from the congested streets in contact with nature. They wanted to know how to build such domes, how to make them, to calculate and design them, although most of them had not even gotten into high school, let alone finished one.

My young friend Michael Ben-Eli, who has worked with me with students in Africa and other places around the world, was able to teach these people and work with them so that after four months they actually acquired spherical trigonometry and were building their own geodesic domes.

The CHARAS group, as a prototype operation of human beings, caught on intuitively that they are really endowed from birth with great intellectual capabilities and they can really employ them, even though they did not go through school. They are able suddenly to master environmental controlling and to realize that they are going to make the breakthroughs. Instead of knocking other people down, with the false idea that "somebody's got to die so that I can live," the kids and the gangs in the streets of New York are becoming spontaneouslay aware—literate and confident—that there is enough to go around for everybody—that it's got to be *you and me*. The movement is in the streets, and it is wonderful news for humanity. The people I see in CHARAS are beautiful people, and their work is the best news I know.

20

—1973

The Event

The Event
Syeus Mottel

It was 1964 and there was a stirring in the land. We had the dream and the shock of the New Frontier. We were now being promised the Great Society. And some earnestly wanted to believe that there was hope.

Two young men, Carlos Garcia (known as Chino) and Angelo Gonzalez, Jr., had known the squalor and degradation of being poor in a rich land. Their anger and energy had pushed them into the gang-oriented world of the Lower East Side of Manhattan.

Chino, at twelve, had joined the Assassins that dominated the Chelsea area of Lower West Side Manhattan. Angelo was the recognized leader. It did not take long before Chino had become the "war lord" responsible for arbitrating or organizing the endless number of rumbles with the Sportsmen gang and others. A born leader who had dropped out of school at the ninth grade without the ability to read or write, he was good at getting people to listen to him. Soon, after meeting Angelo (another gang leader in the Houston Street and East River Section of the Lower East Side), Angelo had Chino establish a younger division of the Dragons. The group became the feared Assassins of First Street and the Lower East Side. Together they soon numbered nearly eight hundred young men and their attending girls.

In their early teens they had become hardened to the street life of their area. They knew how to hustle. Very little was sacred or of consequence to them. To survive was their only credo. And survive they did—through gang wars, reform schools, police harassment, and the neglect of society. Whatever dirt was being handed out, they, somehow, withstood it.

In November of 1964, Chino and Angelo met again at a party. Chino had returned from Puerto Rico. Angelo had returned from Coxachie Prison in upstate New York. It had been suggested that Chino remove himself from the streets of New York for a year. The suggestion had been offered by the New York Police Department. There had been too many incidents that led the police to believe that Chino had become a definite threat to them, others in the community, and to himself.

Angelo had been convicted of an attempted murder charge and had done three years in Coxachie prison. He knew he was a marked man. Any nonsense now would put him away for a long time. He wanted his new freedom to be undisturbed. He had done a lot of thinking in jail. But here was the street again. The streets were dirty, the people uncared for, spirit was lacking, and it was an easy place to "nod out" of the misery and hopelessness. Drugs had begun to dominate the lives of many people Angelo and Chino knew.

They wanted to move into the "tomorrow" of their lives, rather than the violence of yesterday or the emptiness of the "now" that they saw around them. People on TV and the radio were talking about the "Great Society," and they wanted in. So they began to talk. For days, weeks, it seemed to go on forever. Each time they met, Chino or Angelo brought another friend who then brought his. It was like a pyramid club. And they all talked about how they could begin remaking their lives to join this new thing called a "Great Society."

They first formed a romantic idea of organizing a mercenary army to invade Cuba. This idea slowly was replaced with thoughts of how they could—constructively—do something about the poverty and delinquency around them. They were now beginning to call themselves the Real Great Society because that was what they really wanted to be: really great.

Angelo had met a young man named Mike Good who worked as a counselor at Bonitas Youth Services, a neighborhood settlement house. Mike had been a disillusioned college dropout. He had found a sense of purpose on the Lower East Side. It was not long before Mike had turned over his apartment on East 6th Street to Angelo, Chino and the new members of the Real Great Society. He recognized the basic energy and skill of Chino and Angelo. Both had been gang leaders and were now using their old talents and techniques to persuade other gangs to join them. But this time it was to live, not fight over inconsequential turf. Now they wanted to fight the real enemies: poverty, poor housing, lack of education, alienation, and the inadequacy of work skills or the opportunity to learn any. These were their true enemies and they wanted solutions.

Mike helped them realize their full leadership capacity. Chino and Angelo, as gang leaders, in essence had organized small corporate states. Each member had specific duties and responsibilities and was held accountable. Why not do the very same now, but change the orientation and eventual goal? Mike called his brother Fred to join him. Fred had completed two years in the army as a lieutenant and was now thinking of becoming a painter. He was really at loose-ends, but had developed a knack for writing proposals to foundations for support.

The apartment on East 6th Street overflowed with people and activity. Mike and Fred asked the landlord to give them the entire building as a headquarters. To everyone's amazement, the landlord agreed. Fred now fervently worked sorting the vast accumulation of paperwork and details of the bureaucratic world. This approach to problem-solving was very new to all of the Lower East Siders. They usually resolved their problems with a fist, knife or gun. Words on paper and columns of numbers were a new bag. But they held together and learned. They also failed and learned from the failures.

The years between 1964 and 1968 were engrossing and varied for the RGS members. Dr. Charles Slack, of Harvard, became RGS's publicity director and arranged speaking engagements for them around the country. They spoke to kids in Albuquerque, inmates at Alabama State Prison, a psychologists' convention in Philadelphia, criminology classes at the University of Wisconsin—wherever and to whoever would listen to their story, or wanted to pick their brains about the stress and tensions of living in ghettos of poverty and social neglect. They were becoming celebrities; newspapers, magazines and TV covered their excursions across the country and their early activities on the Lower East Side. At this time, they had little to offer except a concept of a new life-force for the usually negative elements of under-privileged and disillusioned youth of center-city areas. There was great flux among the members. Some felt there was too much talk and running around the country, that the basic issues of the ghetto were not being resolved. But Chino and Angelo and a hearty few continued. To their great surprise, a man running an Office of Economic Opportunity (OEO) program in Virginia joined them when his program was phased out because of local racial prejudice. Bill Watman volunteered his aid and soon teamed up with Fred Good to form the official foundation-support and application-writing team. They sent out applications to twenty foundations and the Office of Economic Opportunity in Washington. There was hope that with financial assistance, they could begin active programs on the Lower East Side and ease their constant money problem.

Mountains of paper began to flood the apartment on East 6th Street. Sorting and filing application forms and correspondence became a constant task. The boys from the street stood about in amazement and bewilderment at the activities and drive of Bill and Fred. Here were two white dudes wanting to help them without any ax to grind. This was not like the world they had grown up knowing.

It was not until January, 1967 that they first saw any results from this avalanche of paperwork. The Vincent Astor Foundation came through with $15,000 to support RGS' desire for small business prospects. By beautiful coincidence, RGS' non-profit charter from the State of New York arrived at about the same time. Suddenly, they were in business for real. The Real Great Society was now a tangible entity. And the young men were determined to make a success of this new opportunity. They carefully scrutinized every venture proposed to them as if they were General Motors handing out a franchise. They wanted as many diverse business enterprises they felt they could handle and that could become successful. A discotheque called the Fabulous Latin on 14th Street, a leather shop on Avenue A, a Blimpies Base on the East Side, a boutique on Upper Broadway, and a Westinghouse teaching machine on 6th Street that would be open to the public were just some of the business ventures.

In 1967, one of the RGS' most ambitious plans was initiated. It is still in progress. They opened storefront schools for teaching reading and basic math in East Harlem and the Lower East Side. There were soon over 800 registered students and faculty enrolled in the University of the Streets. Classes were on a one-to-one basis or in small informal gatherings at the various storefronts or at students' apartments. Everything from calculus to origami was being taught. It was inspiring to see the zeal and interest of both students and teachers. School was never like this, nor was the incentive ever more evident.

With all the activity—success and failure—of the 1964–68 period, Chino and Angelo never lost sight of basic problems that affected the Lower East Side. It was these very problems that had pushed them into gangs and crime. These same problems were now causing many of their sisters and brothers to use drugs and to become victims of all the evils of addiction. They realized that housing was basic to the cause and effect of life patterns. The housing on the Lower East Side, by and large, consists of substandard slum buildings and neglected properties owned by absentee landlords. Projects began to dot the streets of the Lower East Side, but many of these soon became depressed areas and prime targets for crime and drugs. New concepts of housing had to be investigated and new lifestyles had to be implemented to make the new conditions work.

The RGS members had, all along, worked as house painters, electricians, plumbers, carpenters, and general fix-it operators to support themselves and their activities. But no concerted programs were ever really started. They attempted organizing a contracting business but soon discovered they did not have the business expertise for commercial competition. They also began working with an East Harlem civic group interested in developing its own co-op housing. This enterprise reached fruition long after RGS' initial influence and presence ended. But most significantly, because of Fred Good's curiosity, Chino came across the name of R. Buckminster Fuller. He had heard that Bucky had very different ideas about the problems of housing and the human condition. Maybe it was the outlaw in Chino (for he had known what it was like to be outside established society) and the basic individualism of Bucky's ideas (also very much outside the usual path of society) that made the first impressions.

28

In March of 1968, Fred made contact with Bucky and asked if he would come and speak to RGS. To his great surprise, Bucky consented eagerly. A large group of people from the Lower East Side gathered in a bare loft on East 7th Street. They came to listen to a New England WASP who spoke in an accent they did not quite understand, and in language and images that were foreign to most of them. The gaps of culture, education, generation, condition, and awareness were inescapable. Yet, a magical thing occurred. Although many of those present did not understand what Bucky was saying, they did listen intently.

Bucky talked to them about man's technological growth and development. Quickly, the RGS people and friends came to understand that Bucky was not another white bureaucrat talking stop-gap social programs. Bucky was talking to them (as he does with all his audiences) about fundamental changes that must occur throughout the world. He was talking about the development of a world community.

This struck home to his audience. They were deeply concerned about creating greater community involvement and awareness among their own people of the Lower East Side. They had realized it was, somehow, necessary to begin with the microcosm of their own neighborhood before approaching the macrocosm of the whole system. Bucky's words and images touched their aspirations for a world based on true equality and plenty.

This short man, in his black suit, looked like a bank clerk or nondescript math teacher rather than an inspiring figure. His white crew cut, heavy-lensed black framed glasses and hearing aid were strange sights to the casually dressed, awkward and, at times, restless audience. Most of them had little formal education or exposure to conceptual thinking. But here was this different little man spilling forth words at an incredible speed, telling them they were part of the entire world system.

He was making them believe their existence was not a question of chance but, rather, a question of choice. Bucky was telling them they could do whatever they wanted, if they wanted and worked at it hard enough. This was not pollyanna political rhetoric he was giving them but hard thoughts of constructive perception. He was trying to imply they were not victims, but potential victors. Bucky was saying that the current system demanded survival of the fittest. He envisioned a new system based upon anticipatory knowledge of a problem, researching the problem, and then coming up with a design to solve the problem on a global basis. He was telling them it was more important to reform the environment than to reform men. Men, he believes, will follow the environmental change and improve.

His concept of doing more with less was at the very root of all of his thinking. People didn't need vast wealth to change things affecting them. What they needed were skills to make these changes. He was saying that their own experiences were wealth (his definition of wealth being energy directed by knowledge) and, therefore, they could learn from each other.

Somehow, they knew he was saying something very important to them and to many beyond themselves. They felt his truth and genuineness. The group caught his enthusiasm and energy. They felt his vibes, and it felt good.

He talked for five hours. No one had ever talked to them that long in their collective experience. He talked to them as equals and as fellow contributors to a new direction. By the time this first session ended, Bucky had acquired a devoted group of travelers on "Spaceship Earth."

The people who were later to form CHARAS listened to R. Buckminster Fuller more intently than the rest, and began to see their world in a different fashion. He opened new areas in their minds and hearts. Now they wanted these spaces filled. They would later begin work on planning and building the domes that Bucky had long ago conceived and designed. The dome, as a structure, was important in changing many of man's attitudes towards building anything. The dome, more importantly, is an introduction to the whole system of thought that Bucky has developed for man's survival and utopian technological growth that can then set man free from needless drudgery. For months afterwards, some of those who had heard Bucky continued their own discussions and "rap" sessions. Very soon, a small band of six seemed committed. They decided they wanted to work independently of the RGS operation. And so CHARAS was created as an acronym and as a concept.

Chino Garcia, Humberto Crespo, Angelo Gonzalez, Roy Battiste, Anthony Figueroa, and Sal Becker. Six young men who had a bond of childhood poverty, neglect, street life, gang warfare, drugs and crime, aimlessness and spiritual depression banded together to find new paths for themselves and the small world around them. They didn't know where they were going, but they knew they did not want to stay where they were. In the writings and philosophy of Bucky and related thinkers, they began to discover a new direction that had cohesion and purpose.

They talked endlessly. They joined Outward Bound, a survival training program, and traveled to Mexico together. They tested their own strength and faith and that of the others. They lived together, goofed together, worked together, cooked meals together, partied together, and talked constantly. At this period, they had met with Ed Schlossberg, an associate of Fuller, who spent time rapping about his systems of thought and inquiring into the thinking processes of the six of CHARAS, and whoever else was around to listen. Finally, they decided it was time to ask Bucky to come and talk to them again. It was early 1969 when Bucky came and talked further with these young men and their friends. He now suggested that they involve themselves in dome-building projects. They accepted the idea eagerly but confessed their ignorance.

Bucky then asked his assistant, Michael Ben-Eli, to go to New York and develop a program with CHARAS. Michael intended to introduce the CHARAS group to dome mathematics and thinking. Michael was an Israeli architect completing his Ph.D. at the Brunel University in London but spending nearly all his time with Bucky and his varied projects. He was very systematic in his approach. Michael introduced the blackboard to his sessions as a vital teaching tool. This quickly turned off many of those present. A blackboard was reminiscent of very bad days in school. But Michael persevered and so did many of the CHARAS group. They had their good days and bad days. Without any money, equipment or regular meeting place, Michael and the group struggled for a year of intense effort.

Chino, who had learned to read and write when he was nearly twenty, had difficulty following the mathematics of dome building. But he understood its impact, and held on. Angelo had developed a very involved marital existence and was constantly being drawn away. Humberto, who was active in hustling anything the group needed and really grooving with the mechanics of dome building, died in a car crash in Maryland while helping a junkie friend go through a cold-turkey period. Anthony was getting more and more caught up in his new career as an artist and actor. Sal met a young lady at one of the sessions. They soon married and he very strongly felt the responsibility of supporting his wife and expected child. Roy, who had a background in IBM computer repair work, remained steadfast. He quickly learned the concepts of spherical trigonometry, solid geometry, and dome math. Although his personal life was not all that secure or well-regulated, Roy devoted himself to working with Michael and attracting new people to CHARAS.

By early 1970, Roy had been able to obtain open loft space in a condemned building owned by the city. So at 303 Cherry Street, CHARAS finally found a semi-permanent home, courtesy of the

Housing and Urban Development Corp. of New York City for a token rental of five dollars per month. It was here that Roy and others were to live together and work on their dome-building training and planning.

Michael, who was traveling between London and the U.S. on what seemed like a shuttle system, kept up a running dialogue with Roy and Chino, his studies in London and activities with Bucky in Carbondale. He soon began clocking as many hours in the air as Bucky did. The amazing thing about this period was that Michael had extremely limited income to do all that he was doing. Yet, somehow, it was getting done.

The young men of CHARAS who lived at, or came through 303 Cherry Street, began implementing their training with two domes that they created out of canvas and two-by-fours. They created two distinct and unusual work spaces. The transformation of open loft space to dome interiors was astonishing. Despite the fact that they had no hot water, heat was irregular in winter and there were no bath facilities, a whole lifestyle began to emerge from this location. The number of people who came through seemed to be endless. This included local community people of all possible interests as well as "uptown" people and dome "freaks" from all over the country who became aware of CHARAS' involvement with Bucky and Michael.

In the fall of 1970, Barry Cohen, of the Environmental Research Center of the School of Visual Arts, heard of the activities of CHARAS. He visited the loft and said he was immensely impressed. He invited CHARAS to become the resident group at his new division at the School of Visual Arts. CHARAS was active at the Center through the Spring of 1971. In February, 1971, CHARAS was a prime exhibitor at the Waldorf-Astoria Hotel convention of the New York Board of Trade, dealing with Recycling Day celebrations in New York City.

Roy became a part-time instructor at the School of Visual Arts during this period. But CHARAS itself was not receiving any form of support. The loft and its upkeep became the individual responsibility of those living there. The activities of CHARAS in the planning and/or building of any domes became CHARAS' own financial problem. Michael, Roy, and others in CHARAS had devised a plan for a sixty-foot dome they wished to erect as an experimental structure somewhere in upper New York state. It was CHARAS' intention to use this dome in a place where the people of the Lower East Side could go and discover that trees grew freely and air was clean.

Because at the media exposure due to the School of Visual Arts involvement and the Waldorf-Astoria Hotel appearance, specific attention was finally directed at the activities of CHARAS. Michael and Roy had been pursuing the construction of cardboard domes as an instant answer to disaster area housing or as an inexpensive mold for ferro-cement domes. To aid them in the financing of this project, an application to the New York State Council on the Arts was submitted. The request was for $15,000 for a year. The application was sent to the Council in May, 1971. It was not until December, 1971 that CHARAS received the first installment. In the interim period, to continue and exist, money was borrowed from Bucky. This money was used to publish a pamphlet on the activities of CHARAS and to order the cardboard dies from the Container Corporation of America. For reasons both practical and emotional, it was decided that the domes should be first built in NYC. It was these dies that CHARAS used to erect their first experimental ferro-cement dome in the East 90s of Manhattan during December, 1971. The site was to be used eventually for urban development. Caught up in all kinds of political wrangles, the site was lying empty. A group sponsored by the Parks Council of New York City and the Vincent Astor Foundation was using the land, later known as Ruppert Green, to present a number of events highlighting ways in which city life could be made more diverse and interesting on a local neighborhood basis. The basic idea was to show how urban space could be converted to make it accessible and useful to the people of the vicinity.

CHARAS was asked to participate. Michael and Roy thought it an excellent idea. They could now test the mold structure and work procedures under actual conditions. What they did not expect was some of the coldest weather New York City had had for some time. The CHARAS group preassembled the geodesic forms and fitted them together at the Ruppert Green site. In three days, despite the cold December weather, the dome was completed.

The entire neighborhood became intrigued with the project. Many stood around in the cold observing the activities involved in the erection of this strange-shaped object. Many more came forward and asked if they could help. People who passed the site on the first day of work, a Friday, and were told they could help in any way they wanted to, rushed home to change their clothes and returned to work late into the night. The same spirit continued over the weekend. It was more a festival than a work crew. Even the bitter cold did not deaden the excitement of all the participants—those in CHARAS and the casual neighborhood people. The entire event became an expression of communal enjoyment and fulfillment.

It was at this same time that the Council funding became available. The request for funds specifically eliminated any provisions for salaries. Roy felt he wanted people's involvement to be based on their willingness to cooperate and function rather than the money derived from their efforts. Beyond the monies needed for equipment and materials, the only funds set aside for the people of CHARAS were a budget for the purchase of food supplies. As Roy remembered saying, "We may be able to manage everything else, but eating is important."

Now CHARAS dug into the work of preparing for the planning of a sixty-foot dome. Michael and Roy spent many long days working out the mathematics of this complicated structure. It was not until the summer of 72 that they realized this dome was too difficult for the group to handle. They needed more experience in the basic aspects of dome building. The idea of dome dwellings as an alternative form of low-income housing needed more investigation.

Behind the loft building serving as CHARAS' headquarters, there were open blocks that had been razed for eventual low-income project development. CHARAS requested permission from the city and the Housing and Urban Development Corporation to use one of these sites as their own experimental testing area. It was hoped that a dome could be erected and left standing for two years to test its durability under all weather conditions and urban stress. The dome that was built at the Ruppert Green was, unfortunately, torn down to allow for that site's development.

All the necessary permissions were granted. CHARAS planned to design and build two small domes at South and Jefferson Streets on the Lower East Side. Both domes would have a 20-foot diameter. One would be a hemisphere and the other a 3/4 of a sphere. with 10 and 15 foot heights respectively, it was thought that under disaster conditions, a family of four could live in either dome shelter. Also, the advantage of being able to erect a complete dome in three days of full effort could make it highly desirable. The eventual cost of such a dome, if produced in mass, would not exceed $500 to $600. No other stable structure could be built so efficiently and inexpensively. Therefore, Michael and Roy felt the need to continue in this direction rather than further pursue the sixty-foot dome idea. There was also the very practical consideration that the funding from the New York State Council on the Arts did not allow for such a grand-scale project.

Throughout all this time, life at the loft on Cherry Street continued developing its own particular style. Luis Lopez was now living there full-time, as well as Roy. Luis worked at the Communications Division of Columbia University and was responsible for all the equipment that was used by the students. He enjoyed his work and had a positive outlook towards all around him. Sometime after Luis moved into the loft, Wilfred Lopez (not a relative) also moved in. Everyone called Wilfred

"Beaver." He was quiet and kept to himself a great deal but was always available whenever work was to be done. Beaver had dropped out of college and was undecided about his future. The fourth occasional resident was James Echevarria. He lived with his family in the Bronx but was spending more time downtown than uptown. He had become Roy's friend sometime earlier. James had seen Roy through some difficult personal times and had developed a strong sense of responsibility to Roy and the activities of CHARAS. He became, in time, CHARAS' most involved member and associate.

There was also a constant flow of other young men and women who came to hangout or work. To many who came to the loft, it was an oasis in an otherwise hostile city. Here people talked to each other. They enjoyed the quiet pleasure of listening to music or "goofing" time away. There were few pressures exerted or felt from the people at the loft. At times, the atmosphere seemed to be one of a continuous low-ebb party. Whenever it got too relaxed, someone would see to it that the chores got done or that work was assigned on an open time schedule. This whole situation was very conducive to many of those who came to the loft with only "street life" patterns as their background. It made consistent efforts a little difficult, but never totally slowed ongoing activities. An indirect, stoic, even cynical attitude pervaded most of the people. "Gung-ho" attitudes would not be received strongly by any of the people at the loft. Yet, when they had to put in 12 to 15 hours of continuous work in impossible weather conditions, they did it. And they did it with humor and good "vibes" at all times.

As is easily discernable, the whole structure of CHARAS is based upon volunteer participation. The organizing and sustaining of such a group is not easy. There are years of implanted negativism that must be overcome, or at least minimized. The aspect of positive goal orientation and achievement are dynamic problems. Chipping away at this erosion is a debilitating and exhausting process. Most of those involved with CHARAS had come from a negative life circumstance and little was expected in their present life relationships, so little was attempted. The continuity of action towards recognizable ends is not easily achieved in this general environment.

During the late winter and early spring of 72 Michael and Roy worked on the many details needed to be solved in anticipation of summer dome building on the site around the corner from the loft. Michael was very excited about working out a new mathematical truncation for the dome design. Such a calculation had never been attempted before. Roy was interested in working the ferro-cement more efficiently than they had at the Ruppert Green site.

Earlier in the year, Michael had met John Deline, a young paper-board manufacturer whose company, Container Systems, is in Denver. Once Michael had resolved the math problems, he went out to Denver to experiment with the new sections and designs for the dies. Deline offered Michael the full use of the experimental facilities at his new plant. When all specifications were ready, it was decided that it would be more convenient to have the paper-board sections produced nearer New York. The order was then placed with Container Corporation in Philadelphia to build the dies and to cut the new sections. Shipment was expected in May. Building would start in June. That seemed to be a reasonable schedule. But Container Corporation soon informed CHARAS that they had serious problems with their cutting machines. The size of each triangular piece (approximately a 3' triangle) was slightly too large for their machinery to hold the running roll of cardboard which had to be held down with enough tension to allow for exact cuts. Michael traveled down to their Philadelphia factory several times to discuss the problem with the company engineers. The dates for the shipments was now pushed up to July. Further technical problems were discovered, and the shipments did not arrive until late August and early September.

Roy's problem of trying to keep the various CHARAS participants involved and concerned during the summer months was very difficult.

It was at this time that one of Roy's brothers was found floating dead in a neighborhood pool, very soon after another brother was seriously wounded in a knife fight. Roy's personal existence was very heavy. James had heard about Roy's unfortunate circumstances, and came downtown to spend some time with his buddy, who had become very withdrawn. James got a car and a jug of cognac and took Roy into the country for a week or so. They just roamed throughout upper New York State. James allowed Roy to work out his grief, anger and despair, without intrusion or advice. He was just there to be a friend. They traveled about getting high and falling out wherever they happened to stop. After a week or so, Roy said it was time to get back to the city and work. James returned to the loft with Roy, and found he had become a member of CHARAS without realizing he had embarked upon a new life direction.

As the cardboard triangles began arriving, small work crews assembled them into diamond shaped sections. Each piece had scored flaps that were folded to form a triangular box. Four such triangular boxes formed the diamond pre-assembled "wall" section. The sections were held together by bolts. It all fitted together like a marvelously devised jigsaw puzzle.

Right: James and Michael assembling paper board sections.

Two domes were planned to nestle in the southeastern section of the open site. Each dome was expected to be completed in three days of work. Roy's major concern was having enough people to function effectively. He knew he had the able assistance of James, Luis, Beaver and Chino. Each, in turn, would be asking friends of his to join them in their efforts. There were also many young people from the neighborhood, such as Roberta Fulton and Matty Small, who could be depended upon. Beaver's friend, Felix Almodova, was eager to assist. Tony Guitard, Roy's friend from the Bronx, would be faithful. Jose Cordero, Chino's friend who every one called "Brother Marx" (of the Marx Brothers, that is), stated he would commit his full time to get the domes up. David LaTouche and David Lorenzano, from the Children's

Art Workshop on 6th Street, said they would be available. Mark Spagnola, who lived in Jersey and met Roy at the School of Visual Arts, would be around when needed. Al Santana said he and his car would be at CHARAS' disposal whenever he was free. And so it went. A loosely knit network of workers began to form.

Right: Sections are assembled into diamond patterns by Roy.

The assembly of the diamond sections for the two domes progressed slowly during late September and early October. Roy wanted a fairly pleasant day to begin the work on the smaller dome but the weather was very erratic. Most days it was cold, with impending rain.

The word went out. Tuesday morning, October 31st at 9 A.M., the diamond sections were transported from the fourth-floor work loft to the building site around the corner. Maneuvering the sections down the stairwells was not an easy task. Several sections were dented and one light fixture was neatly chopped off by one of the wing-like sections. The darkened stair area made movement even more precarious. But all the sections were finally out on the field by two in the afternoon. Many of the sections resembled giant turtles lying on their backs while basking in the sun. Several days before, Roy, Michael, James and some of the neighborhood kids had cleared two circular spaces and covered and leveled them with gravel. They then laid down a circle of two-inch planking that had been painted with creosote, a water-resistant sticky liquid. When the sections were prepared for assembly, the wood was dry and ready. The first diamond section was raised in place and bolted into the wood base. Everyone stood back and admired the section standing strong and resolute. There it was. The beginning of a dome on the Lower East Side.

Work progressed evenly through the long afternoon and well into the evening. It was not until midnight that the dome would be completed and covered with its polyethylene film sheeting as protection against rain.

Everyone worked with quiet and good-humored ease. When he didn't know what to do, he asked. No one demanded a break or

complained about the long hours and the increasing nighttime cold. There was no additional light to work with during the long evening hours except some weak flashlights. Yet the work went on until the last section was in place and securely bolted to its adjoining section. It all fit together. The mathematical calculations were correct and the building schematic had been properly drawn. Michael and Roy modestly congratulated themselves.

Shortly before the last section had been fit in place, Matty and Roberta came onto the site and announced that they had cooked an enormous dinner for everyone. Most had not eaten all day or evening. Some wine had been passed around in the early evening but it went very quickly. Roy turned to Anthony, after the girls made their announcement, and invited him to join the dinner feast. He was pleased to accept.

Assembly of the dome attracted Anthony to join the effort.

Anthony Revelli, a carpenter's helper who lived further up FDR Drive, had come by the site at about four in the afternoon on his bicycle. He had stopped to observe the guys working. He then rode on. Soon he was back, edging closer to the fence for a better view. He rode off again, but in a few minutes he was back. He had become intrigued with whatever it was that was happening inside the fence. He finally asked one of the guys what was going on. When he was told that a geodesic dome was being built, he was incredulous. "Who's paying you guys to do this," he wanted to know. He was told it was all volunteer labor. Now he looked really surprised. "You mean to say you guys have been out here all day without any bread?" He was assured that no one was getting paid. He wanted to know who was in charge. Roy came forward and was introduced. Anthony wanted to know if CHARAS was a profit-making organization. He was told it was not. "Then, man, can I help, too?" He finally left the loft (after he, along with everyone else, had enjoyed the delicious dinner that Matty and Roberta had prepared) well after 2 A.M., feeling he had made some friends, and had participated in something real.

The exhaustion that everyone felt that evening and the next day was mingled with a sense of pride. A dome shelter stood on the Lower East Side. An impossible feat had been achieved. Business and government had long talked about the feasibility of dome structures for general use. But except for a few prime exceptions, Bucky's dome structures were still an oddity in the architectural vocabulary. But here on the Lower East Side of Manhattan, a group of ex-gang members, ex-junkies, criminals, and neighbors had created a moment of history.

Early Thursday morning, it began to rain. Many people who had worked Tuesday arrived at the loft without being called. They all wanted to know what could they do if the dome was going to be threatened by the rain. A second polyethylene sheet was quickly purchased and pulled over the existing sheeting. Each sheet of polyethylene measured 40 feet by 100 feet. As wind reached under the sheet, it bellowed up and formed a giant sail. It was not easy to secure this sheeting in the rain and the wind, but after nearly two hours, all was fastened down. Everyone retreated to the loft space to dry out and warm up.

It was not until the following Monday, November 6th, that the weather was good enough to begin work on the second larger dome. On the previous Friday, a *New York Times* reporter appeared and interviewed Michael, Roy, and Chino rather taciturnly. The story appeared on the next to last page of the Saturday, November 4th issue. That Saturday became visitor's day. Michael had brought some business types down to see the small dome. Others, who had read the story in the *Times*, dropped by all afternoon. Suddenly, anyone who was involved with the dome building of the prior Tuesday and was present, became a guide and explainer of CHARAS, geodesic domes, Bucky Fuller's philosophy, and other whys and wherefores. The site took on the atmosphere of a country fair.

Again, on this Monday, the diamond sections had to be carried down from the fourth-floor work loft to the site. Actual piecing together of the preassembled sections did not begin until early afternoon. While this was happening, a car drove up to the site and a man strode across the field wanting to know who was in charge. He had a calm but official manner about him. He was Joseph Stein, Commissioner of Housing for the City of New York. He, too, had read the *Times* article and was curious if a building permit had been obtained by CHARAS. Michael and Roy stated they had intended doing so but just hadn't gotten around to it. The Commissioner seriously suggested that a visit to his office would find his staff very receptive and understanding. He understood the experimental nature of the project. He merely wanted CHARAS to be protected against eventualities possible without the official permit. Everyone thanked everyone and the Commissioner left. The long arm of officialdom had finally reached out and touched CHARAS. They had to subscribe to the rules and regulations, no matter how different they wanted their lifestyle to be or their concepts for tomorrow were. It was an interesting confrontation for everyone involved.

The building of the second dome proceeded without hitch or problem. Because of delays, again, the dome was not complete until late at night. This time, someone was able to rig an auto headlight to storage batteries for some illumination. There was nothing to be done about the cold. The night temperatures plunged downward to the mid 20s.

It was rough, but the six CHARAS people worked through the long hours with absolutely no bitching about anything. The need to complete the dome superseded their discomfort.

The events of the day did not go unrecorded. CBS-TV News sent Lynn Sherr and a film crew to check out the dome building. They spent about an hour filming and interviewing various CHARAS people that were around. As it turned out, only the silent film footage was used with Ms. Sherr's commentary. It appeared on the 6 P.M. news. Interestingly enough, no one who was working on the dome broke the work schedule to go to the loft and view the program.

Tuesday was another day of exhaustion for everyone. The consensus around the loft was that they had to start earlier in the day so that the arduous night work could be avoided. The combination of little or no light and extreme cold made such working conditions very difficult.

Late Tuesday night it began to rain. By Wednesday, the rainfall had reached 5.2 inches, a record rainfall. The entire city was affected. Subways were stalled. There were blackouts in sections of Brooklyn and Queens. New York was totally wind-swept and rain-sogged.

When Roy went out to check the domes at 10:30 A.M, he discovered that various sections of the two domes were severely stressed due to water leakage. The polyethylene had cracked along the staple punctures holding the sheeting in place. Roy immediately went off to order more polyethylene sheeting. Once he had called his supplier, he went back to the site and propped up the sagging walls with lengths of lumber. It wasn't until 3 P.M. that the sheeting was delivered. At the same time, David LaTouche and his friend Christopher Miller came driving up to the site. With Roy, they fought the wind and the rain. Covering the smaller dome was not that difficult. But the larger dome presented many problems. Wooden triangular window sections had been placed into the large dome. The wind had ripped at the plastic sufficiently to allow the wood edges to cut through. To pull the plastic sheeting over the girth of the dome, with record winds of more than 50 miles per hour tugging at them and the rain pouring down, made the entire situation hazardous and very tough. The rain formed large pools of water on the sheeting, adding enormously to its weight and difficulty of handling.

It took four and a half hours to complete the salvage job on the two domes. Everyone was drenched. Once back at the loft, clothes were peeled off and hung to dry. The loft took on the air of a large laundry room at a Turkish bath. Everyone sat around in the nude waiting for his clothes to dry. Some tea was brewed and drunk. No one really talked. Everyone felt too tired and miserable. What also gnawed at everyone was the fear of permanent damage to the dome structures. Slowly, as clothes dried enough to be worn, everyone left the loft to Roy and his obvious doubts and worries.

Michael became sick from the battle with the elements. He had come down to the site wearing nothing but a thin cotton jacket under a 99-cent plastic raincoat and a polka dot rain hat. He looked ludicrous and gave everyone the laugh that was needed. When the sun finally came out on Friday, Roy gave Michael his telephone report. The domes were not totally destroyed. True, some of the sections had to be replaced. But the structure was basically sound. The smaller dome was harder hit than the larger, and needed more replacement panels. Michael quickly suggested that new cardboard triangles be ordered from Container Corporation. Roy laughed quietly. He had just received the bill from Container. CHARAS' bank account did not have the money to cover that bill, if it were to be paid immediately. Michael recommended that the order be placed anyway. They would worry about paying the bills at some other time. The important object now was to repair the domes and get them ready for the ferro-cementing procedures.

The following week was a combination of bad weather, Michael suddenly having to fly to London for a week, Roy getting involved with some local art groups that were forming an association for easier funding, and general ennui on the part of many of the people who hung around the loft. Tuesday of that week, another 1.61 inches of rain fell, further weakening the domes. More lumber was brought in to prop up newly discovered sags. It was soon evident that the sealer which Container had used on the corrogated cardboard was not very water resilient. By Friday, Roy decided it was imperative that the large dome be dismantled and reassembled with the excess triangles on hand. James and Roy did this job through the weekend by themselves. Very few of the usual crew showed. There seemed to be a feeling of desertion. Again, on Sunday, the rain was pretty heavy and the endless job of getting the plastic cover over the domes was again performed.

At about 10:30 P.M., Roy took his dog out for a walk and to check on the condition of the domes. As he turned the corner of Cherry Street, he saw Fire Department trucks parked down the block. A quick sprint brought Roy alongside the fence. The firemen were smashing the small dome into unrecognizable pieces. In his usual stoic state, he entered the field to inquire why this demolition was going on.

Shortly before Roy arrived, a call had been placed to the Fire Department reporting an intensely smoky fire burning at South and Jefferson Streets. Fire Department Company 17 immediately responded. They discovered the small one with heavy smoke billowing out of it. In their overly zealous manner, they started to chop and rip apart the entire plastic-covered cardboard structure.

Apparently, what had occurred was that an unknown person had come into the dome for shelter from the rain and then, very neatly, had built a grate fire-pit. Once the fire started, the smoke could not escape since the dome was fully covered by plastic. In his haste to retreat from this smoke-filled enclosure, the fire was kicked onto some plastic sheeting that had been stored inside the dome. The smoke from the burning plastic became even more profuse. Whoever had entered the dome for the very reason it had been erected, namely shelter, then fled into the soggy night. Up to the point of the Fire Department's arrival, the dome itself was not on fire or in threat of fire.

But there it was. The small dome had been totally destroyed, and, with it, many triangle sections that had been stored inside it. Roy returned to the loft and went to bed.

Michael returned from London late Monday evening and was immediately hit with the news of the dome's loss. On Tuesday, Michael came downtown and conferred with Roy. They would salvage what-ever they could from the destroyed sections. At least, the hardware could be retrieved. James went out to the site and immediately began stripping the destroyed cardboard sections of all their nuts and bolts. That seemed to be the day's activity. Nothing else could be done until the new triangles arrived from the Container plant in Philadelphia.

The next few days dwindled away into idle gatherings of people who just "hung-out." There was more rain over Saturday and Sunday morning. To complicate life further, the heating system at the loft building failed. It became colder inside than outside. Even when the sun broke through on Sunday afternoon, the spirit or willingness to do anything was minimal. By Monday, Roy had come down with a bad case of the flu and was laid out for the next three days. General depression and defeat seemed to be in the air.

Chino met with Roy on the 29th, and word went out that work would be completed on the large dome at the first change in the weather. It was not until December 3rd that the weather turned friendly, with temperatures in the high 60s. It was a lovely day. Work was started on the general repair of the sections so that the first layer of a plastic sheet could be placed as a base for the chicken wire frame. This had to be done before the ferro-cementing could begin.

These activities continued into Monday. The dome was now cov-ered with a plastic shield. It would act as an insulator against any more rain that might fall, and as the necessary base for the cementing. The rest of that week had both good and bad weather. When it was good, people would show up but nothing would get done. Old, persistent feelings of negativism seemed to be evident.

On Monday, December 11th, Michael was leaving for a three-week trip across the United States to visit various citrus juice plants in preparation for a two-year job designing such a plant in Israel. He wanted assurance that work would continue at CHARAS while he was away. He helped Roy set the wood frame for the entrance to the dome. He also had a long talk with Roy and later with Chino via phone. Nevertheless, it was not until ten days later that further work was considered. A cement mixer was picked up from one of the local community groups in anticipation of the next large effort. More days of rain followed. And soon, the Christmas period was upon everyone and only partying seemed to occupy everyone's attention. Two days after Christmas, work on the chicken wire frame was started with Roy and James basically working alone. Sometimes, in the days following, Felix, David or Beaver would be around to help. But it was primarily Roy's and James' show.

And then there was New Year's and more pre-event partying and post-event recovery. Finally, on January 13, a large assembly of people met at the site. The cement-mixer was rolled out of the Cherry Street building, and hooked up to a city lamppost for needed current. In the previous three weeks, in a haphazard fashion, the chicken-wiring and other preparations for the cementing process had been completed. Now, with the cement-mixer whirring at the corner of Jefferson and Water Streets, the last step in the completion of the dome was to be accomplished.

With Michael's return to New York, preparation for final cementing began. Although the weather was really too cold for proper cementing, Roy thought if some antifreeze was mixed in with the water, all would be well. The large group of people who had come to work were festive in their attitude. There was great gusto and humor. David Lorenzano and Raymond Isaacs became the ace top-of-the-dome cementers. They easily and beautifully placed themselves on the very top of the dome and troweled cement quickly and with a sense of expertise that was great to observe. Of course, neither had ever done this before. But, no one would have known. The cry "more cement" kept ringing up from all over the dome.

The exterior of the dome is covered with plastic sheeting, furring strips stapled onto the surface and three layers of chicken wire are applied for cementing to follow.

Work on the dome was moving ahead very rapidly. Even Michael's announcement that he will be getting married in late February, which both pleased and surprised many people, did not stop the work tempo. Michael had to really get his back into the job to keep up with the excellent efforts all around him. Everyone who was there got into the cementing act: men, women, and children. Casual strangers strolling by caught the infectious feeling and asked if they could help.

It got dark early and work had to stop. The dome was covered, once again, with the plastic sheeting. Michael and Roy were very worried whether the next day's cementing would weld well with the prior day's work. Ferro-cementing is usually done as one continuous activity to allow for even curing of the cement surfaces. Well, they had gone this far. They had to take the chance.

The next morning, Sunday, everyone was working at 10 A.M. Christopher Miller became the expert cementer and finisher. He showed extraordinary dexterity at using two trowels simultaneously. Christopher became the envy of all those working. Soon everyone was trying to sneak a second trowel and adopt Christopher's system.

Roy had placed himself at the cement-mixer and worked at

keeping the mixture of water and cement even throughout the two-day period. As had happened before, Michael observed that even without any real organization or visible working plan, everything seemed to be falling into place and functioning well. The fact that everything was going so well was amazing. People came and went during the two days of cementing as they had done previously. One person picked up where another left off. A sense of continuity existed when work was actively approached but the looseness of organization became more evident in the slack periods.

By 1 P.M., when a picnic lunch break in the 30° sunshine was called, it was visibly clear that the dome had been completely cemented except for minor touches. The lunch of sandwiches, milk, soda, and coffee was festive. Every-so-often someone would break from the lunch area, where people sat on the ground, or on boxes, and would slowly circle the dome with sandwich or drink in hand. He would look at the dome with a glow of contentment. Others had a look of sadness as if they would never again have the same feeling of accomplishment and purpose that they had shared during these two days.

Michael and Roy conferred about the potential problem of the two sections of cement joining and curing as one piece rather than crack-ing or totally separating. They decided that keeping the dome surface as wet as possible, for a few days, might solve the problem. They wanted the "seam" of the two sections of cement to be particularly moist to provide greater possible union and cohesion.

Right: Lynn Tiefenbacher, of the Children's Art Workshop, Michael and Christopher Miller busy applying the ferro-cement in the last stages of construction.

The rest of the afternoon had the appearance of many small town squares around the world. People just stood around joking, talking, enjoying the stirs in the brisk cold air, and having a feeling of commonality. They had all, at one time or another, been part of this event. It belonged to none of them and yet, it belonged to all of them. The dome had touched their lives as surely as they had physically created the dome. This somehow made them feel important and together.

Bucky was speaking at Carnegie Hall that evening. When he was told the dome had been completed that very afternoon, he wanted to visit the dome the next day and changed his plans to be free to do so. When the cab, on Monday afternoon, came to a rise on F.D.R. Drive in the vicinity of the site, Bucky asked the driver to slow down so that he could look out at the dome site with ease. Behind his thick lenses, his eyes squinted very carefully as if he were trying to get the dome clearly in sight and not miss a nuance of the topography or construction.

The cab swung onto Jefferson Street and stopped directly across the street from the dome. Bucky climbed out quickly. Slowly and alone, he walked toward the fence. He stood there for a long moment and then turned to the group that had accompanied him. The cab-driver had also gotten out of the car. He must have felt he was seeing something special. Bucky walked back to the group and softly said, "It's beautiful, isn't it?"

There are over 100,000 geodesic domes in the world today. Bucky has designed or supervised the planning and construction of most of them. He has seen domes that rose in one week become concert halls. He has seen domes on Mt. Fuji in Japan and a dome at the Expo 67 in Montreal. But the sense of pride that glowed from him looking at this 15' high, 20' in diameter dome was overwhelming.

Roy and a small band of guys were rounding the corner at Cherry Street. As Bucky noticed them walking towards him, he moved forward to join them. Roy and Bucky greeted each other in the middle of the Water Street thoroughfare, Bucky warmly grasped Roy's hand. The others (Beaver, David Lorenzano, Mark Spagnola, Mark's friend Joe Wider, and two neighborhood kids who just tagged along) clustered around Bucky. Here was the man himself. This was the cause of their holding together for so long. Here was the reason for the change in their lives. This was the man that had affected them very deeply, whether they knew it or not. And here he was being introduced and saying "Bless you," "thank you, thank you," "you must be very proud."

Then Bucky introduced his wife, his secretary, Shirley Swanson, and even asked the cabdriver to introduce himself to everyone.

The gate to the site was unlocked and the entire group crossed the field. Bucky walked up to the dome and patted it gently. Michael mentioned the problem they were expecting concerning the welding of the "seams." Bucky looked at it and said he thought it would work satisfactorily. He walked around the dome very slowly and quietly. He then entered and studied the cardboard interior, He made some comments about the water damage and possible steps to take to prevent it happening again.

"It's a victory, it's a triumph," Bucky said as he emerged from the dome. He made it sound as if they had just completed a Taj Mahal or other monument. His enthusiasm was infectious and boundless. Soon, everyone was laughing, standing around and just talking.

A young man came strolling towards the group. He asked if the structure was a geodesic dome. When told it was, he smiled and said, "I saw it from the highway and had to come over to check it out." He mingled for a few moments. Someone mentioned to him that the old man standing with the young men was Bucky. He looked dumbstruck and mumbled some unintelligible comment. He then rushed over to Bucky and began pumping his arm with fantastic zest. "I don't believe it," he gushed. "Bucky Fuller, really. Wow. I don't believe I'm meeting you and shaking your hand." He then turned away and walked out of the field. The cabdriver, Stavros Yazy, turned to someone and whispered, "Hey, is this man important or something?" He was told some people think he is. "Well, it sure seems so here," he remarked and went to look at the dome more carefully.

Everyone posed for pictures at Bucky's insistence. He made it feel like the opening of an impressive bridge or public building. Everyone, suddenly, had a feeling of importance about himself and the achievement of the dome structure. It wasn't really so extraordinary. But considering where some of these people had come from and where they were now, then, maybe, it was a milestone. This, perhaps, was what Bucky felt and knew. And it was this sense of growth and development that he wanted to communicate and nurture.

The sun was beginning to set, cutting across the Manhattan Bridge, refracting its light into millions of spokes shooting up from the bridge's metalwork. The air was getting chilly. Mrs. Fuller suggested they return to the car. Bucky was reluctant to leave. He was assured by Roy and the others that they appreciated his visit and that they knew he had to leave. Bucky reached out and embraced Roy, Michael, and several others. The warmth of his parting seemed to affect the air. It didn't feel so cold anymore.

The cab pulled away down towards South Street. The CHARAS boys watched the cab disappear into the merging traffic and then they returned to the loft feeling at peace, and for the first time in a long time, at ease. They sank into chairs and couches and just smiled.

53

The New People

James Echevarria

There is a deceptive quality about this lean, sinewy young man. He has the physique of a long distance runner and seems to have the taciturn manner attributed to that athlete. But upon further contact and acquaintance, you discover James Echevarria to be a very disarming and subtly humorous person. His sudden thrusts of ironic wit expose him. There is a very warmhearted man under the straight-faced attitude that is his usual demeanor.

James is comparably new in the CHARAS ranks. Actually, he first came down to the loft on Cherry Street to console his friend Roy Battiste. On July 24, 1972, Roy's brother Orvin was found dead in the Lower East Side Pitt Street Park Pool. July 25 was Roy's birthday. Several days earlier, another brother of Roy's, Peter, was seriously cut up in a knife fight. Both the fight and the death were drug related.

James had been a very good friend of Orvin's. He knew that Orvin's death would be a tremendous blow to Roy. James had befriended Roy when they both lived near each other in the Bronx. James had become "tight" with Roy during many weekend-long parties attended by their brothers, cousins and friends. They shared similar outlooks on life although little was communicated directly. James remembers that those weekends resembled gatherings of a joyous and harmonious family.

Roy had not been involved with the drug culture as directly as had his two brothers. James had one full year of involvement and one year of trying to break out of his "habit." He, therefore, could have stronger sympathy and understanding of Roy's brothers' world and behavior patterns. But he could also have compassion for the agony he believed Roy would be experiencing at the news of his brother's death.

James came to Cherry Street to "hang-out" with a friend during a particularly trying moment. He discovered that Roy wanted to get away from everything. They took off for upper New York State with a jug of cognac and little else. Whatever association these two young men had had previously was to be fully cemented during the week they roamed through the countryside getting high and rediscovering their friendship.

James was born on Welfare Island twenty-four years ago. He grew up in Spanish Harlem and went to school there. He went on to the Food and Maritime High School. James' father, brother, brother-in-law and three out of five uncles were active in the Merchant Marine. It was natural for him to think he wanted to follow in their footsteps.

Most of the time, while growing up, he was alone. His father was usually away and his older brother had little time for him. Later, his brother joined the Merchant Marine, leaving James with his mother and his sister who was fourteen years older than he. Although his mother was strict in his early years, she was not domineering. James, to this day, has a good relationship with his mother and cares for her needs and welfare as best he can.

Whatever contact James had with his father was abruptly ended when he was five and his parents separated. He then found in his cousin, Tony Guitard, the friendship he needed. They lived on the same block and spent over twelve years together on that 119th Street and Second Avenue insular "Barrio" ghetto world.

Entering high school meant going downtown into the foreign and unknown territory of "Anglo" Manhattan. His existence till then had been totally dominated by his neighborhood. A further complication at the beginning of his high school career was that he retained, at fourteen, the baby-faced look of a ten-year-old. The fact that his brother, Alvin, was a senior at the same school, coupled with James' childish appearance and sophomore class standing, meant that Alvin had to virtually ignore his younger brother while school was in session. That one year was very crucial to James. He began to realize that his life was getting to be a serious matter. It was no longer merely getting up in the morning and going to sleep at night and filling the time in between as effortlessly as possible.

James recalls that marijuana was prevalent at about this period. "At first it was getting high for laughter's sake," James says softly. His tone is always confidential and reassuring. "Yeah, we'd get high and goofed all the time. Then came getting high and doing things. Getting high was a secondary thing." James considers what he has just said and a realization dawns upon him. "At first it was get high and do anything. Then it was let's do something. We kind of matured as a group. That is, my brother and cousin Tony."

The feelings of uncertainty that prevailed in his first year of high school caused James to continue the pattern of "goofing" although he was basically a good student. A broad smile escapes as James remembers, "I would always have to come out with jokes. But never any serious trouble. Suspension just once or twice." His smile has now erupted into a self-satisfying laugh. "Yeah, only suspension. For calling a teacher mother-fucker or something. But I got along well with most of my teachers. They saw I had a mind but was just goofing off most of the time."

He managed to squeak through high school and went on to New York Community College in downtown Brooklyn. He was planning to major in hotel and restaurant management. James' previous levity has now become somewhat somber as he talks of that first year. "That first year in Community College was really a struggle. It was really a hassle. The summer after my first year of college, I shipped out aboard a ship to South America. I'd sit out on deck and get high. Be relaxed. Feel so small in an ocean. I had time to think. I'd think, 'Here I am. What am I going to do. Am I going to go back to school and check it out to see if I could do it or cut out and try something else.' Well, I went back to school and it was totally different.

"I was looking for an education now. The first year I waited for people to fill me in on things and to tell me books to read or reports to do. But now I was making decisions about what I wanted to do, what time I was going to spend doing it. I really used the library to the utmost. It was a lot better than waiting about for things. I began to realize you must make things happen for yourself, within yourself. And, slowly, through the succeeding years I have been trying to add to that basic belief."

James astonishes people when he becomes philosophic because it is a portion of his personality that he has only recently been tapping and understanding. His usual aspect is of dogged attention to his work or unexpected flashes of irony.

It is again evident when he describes the period after his graduation from New York Community College. The sparkle of humor is reflected in his eyes and his voice has the lilt of lightheartedness as he says, "Yeah! Got out but I didn't want to get into the hotel industry. I wanted to try something else I was good at—numbers. I had a straight A in accounting. I averaged 98 in Accounting on all the tests combined throughout the two years at N.Y.C.C.

"So I got a job with an import and export house downtown. I worked there for nine months in accounting. But then I didn't know where to go from there. I didn't want to stay in accounting. It seemed every time I tried something I found out I didn't really want to stick with it. Except CHARAS. But that's different and comes later."

James retreats into himself for a moment before going on. He is striving to find the complete image to express his next thought. His face brightens and he continues, "That's why I'm still not set on my career. What gets me is to give twenty years to a career and at the end of it to be able to say 'Alright.' I'd rather live those twenty years and have five or six different short careers and say this way was better."

Without really knowing it, James has expressed one of Bucky Fuller's ideas—the generalist versus the specialist. James has learned this concept through his experience. Again, Bucky believes experience can be your best guide. It is no wonder that James found his way to CHARAS and that Bucky and CHARAS found themselves bound together.

James had met Roy at a Bronx party on Good Friday nearly seven years ago. The young men and women had a "cool night" getting high and feeling the good vibrations that everyone was emitting. Strong impressions were made and Roy and James knew they had become friends although they would not meet again until 69. But by this time James was beginning to snort heroin. His attention span and interest level was very low. He could not concentrate his thoughts or energies except to satisfy his growing habit. Roy was then beginning his intense involvement with Chino and Angelo in formation of CHARAS and his studies with Michael Ben-Eli.

James attended one of these sessions and found it far beyond his capacities.

In the intervening two years, James was to become heavily addicted and then break from his drug entanglement. James is very guarded and resistant when talking about it. He attempts to pretend that that wasted two year period of his life was merely a violent transition in his growth and development. It was his descending into chaos and finding the strength to rise out of the ensnaring trap of drugs that has fashioned James into the thoughtful, concerned and philosophical young man he is now.

"I knew Roy's brother and I really dug him. He used to get high with us. He and Roy weren't on the same level. But they were cool people. Roy didn't agree with the shit Orvin was doing in order to get dope. Then Roy never went through dope to know what that really felt like. I had." The sense of gloom and despair has been apparent on James' face and in his voice as he relates this episode in his past. Sadly, he goes on, "But I dug Orvin. But I also realized that Roy must be going though some heavy trips when I heard Orvin had been killed. So I came down. We hung out together for the next week or so. It was between getting high and running around the countryside of upper New York that Roy began rapping about the three domes he had to put up before the end of the year. And he had problems. He had to do this with the remaining funding he had from the New York State Council. But they hadn't gotten the special cardboard from Container Corporation yet. Roy had to go out to California for a convention on top of everything else. So I just stayed down at the loft and began checking it all out. As to Orvin's death and how Roy reacted, that is something else.

"If you're going to take someone off, you know there is the chance you can get killed. Roy wasn't expecting it but it wasn't a shock. He was very cool about it. Maybe even cruel at times when he would get into a heavy rap with me. But he got over it and knew he had other things to do than to sit around and groan."

It was with this expression of friendly compassion that James entered the daily life and struggles of CHARAS and the imminent dome-building experience. James readily admits, "I didn't really know what I was getting into. I think it was a change in my life. I was not involved too much with anyone or anybody or anything. Except for dope for the one year and the second year to get out of it. Once I was out of it, I started checking everything out. It was like going into high school again saying, 'Wow. This world is opening up.'

"I found that the world was bigger than I actually thought. I began thinking that there were so many things I could do. Just had to find the handle. Then came the encounter with Roy because of his brother. I thought that the construction of the domes would be a tremendous amount of work. It would be easier if I were on hand. The only other people at the loft then were Luis and David. Luis was busy with his work at Columbia and David was just getting out of his drug involvement and drinking a lot and getting high. Just sort of substituting highs. It's the lesser of two evils but still involving your head in getting high. Getting high and enjoying the high rather than doing something. But it seemed he wanted to get involved.

"Chino was in Chicago at some seminar and Angelo was off doing his own thing. So I just stayed to help and work. I began digging the life and energy of the loft. It was a constant meeting of people, people being together. Not only on the job but afterwards. We ate together, goofed together, shared the same sleeping space. Was more open minded. People weren't just hanging out together. They were now looking into each other more. That's what interested me."

James ponders for a moment and then states, "Everybody had the right attitude. I mean everyone doing their share. A feeling of community. Now it wasn't all a bed of roses, friend. When the work slackened because of the shitty weather and destruction of cardboard sections due to the fire in the small dome, then things would slide a little. People would then just want to hang out and groove. It then began to fall heavily on me and Roy. Some of those people began thinking of us as some kind of Lower East Side community group. They make phone calls and eat up all the food. They leave their dirt and dishes behind them not giving a fuck. But, fortunately, we were a close-knit group and everybody would rap to each other. So someone could say, 'Hey man, what are you slopping up,' always with a light-hearted attitude.

"What began to worry me was that a tremendous number of people would be coming up every day. It was becoming less of a business place and more of a hangout. You can't have that. While we were working, everything was cool. But the periods in between became a hassle sometimes.

"People began looking at me as second in command or something. That was not my idea at all. I just happened to be there when Roy had to go to California so I took care of things. Then the cardboard started to arrive. Roy would be outside or upstairs with a group working and I would be inside with another group. Roy would explain what had to be done and when. I then became one who others would come to ask what was needed to be done. What I didn't like was people just sitting around if Roy was not there or someplace else. People would slack off then."

Even though James sees many of the pitfalls and traps of a loosely organized group such as CHARAS, he has not really lost the initial enthusiasm he discovered at 303 Cherry Street. He muses about this and says, "Yeah! There have been times I've thought of going out and buying a couple suits, shirts and ties and getting the ol' resume together and go out looking for a job. But I think that will pull me away from CHARAS. Then I say, 'No.' We can really move this organization if I stay with it. Because Roy and I get along fine. We think fine. I could see my involvement getting deeper. A lot of things would have to be put together better. But I have belief they could be.

"Because CHARAS is not only about dome building. I don't yet know that much about geodesic mathematics. I could learn quick. I have a good head. But CHARAS is more of a lifestyle. It's more about involvement of people who never thought they would be involved in anything or included into anything. Not just in domes but in anything. What I have learned down at the loft hasn't been about domes and geodesics, it's been more about people. What people can do when they feel it is their friendship that is being called on.

"Right now I'm living two lifestyles. One downtown at the loft and, now, living with my mother in a South Bronx low-income project apartment. There are weeks when I'm downtown living as best I can. Then I come uptown to the Bronx and survive doing whatever is available. I'm flexible in my ways. But it would be nice if I could concentrate my energies downtown more. Maybe, in the future, there might be enough money available to see to it that we can exist the way we want to. I have no illusions, only occasional hope. I ask myself the same question every morning, 'How do I keep myself together.' And when I think of CHARAS, I think getting it together is one problem. The major problem is keeping it together."

James has a leadership capacity that has never been fully exercised. He has a grasp of reality that has been chiseled out of extreme pressures. He has developed a vision of tomorrow that could be a glowing example to many more people like him. He can consolidate all of this into a resourceful unit if given a chance to go further. CHARAS may be that vehicle. Or some other similar group may serve this purpose. However it is done, the important consideration is that a valuable asset—James Echevarria—will be lost if the opportunity is not, somehow, made available.

Roberta Fulton

There is always a smile on her face. Her laughter is contagious and full of warmth. Roberta Fulton is now 18. She has witnessed the junkie using his spike and feared the mugger lurking in the hallways of her project building. Yet her eyes still glow with the excitement of one whose dreams have not been shattered. She has a sincerity and eagerness that encourages friendship.

Roberta has known the guys at CHARAS for over a year and feels comfortable and relaxed with them. "Like part of the family... like being their little sister," she says as her smile radiates her warmth. She lives across the street from the loft. From her 16th-story apartment window in the LaGuardia Project she shares with her mother and father, one brother and three sisters, Roberta had often seen Roy riding his bicycle or walking his dog. During the summer of 1972, she had met James quite casually with some friends and was invited to visit the loft. She remembers with fondness her first visit and the discovery of an unexpected, fulfilling experience. "We sat around and talked. You can rap about anything to them. I found them to be nice."

Roberta was told about CHARAS' dome-building plans. She admits she didn't understand all that was happening at the loft. When James asked if she would help with the preparations leading to the building of the dome, she enthusiastically accepted. "I would never have thought something like that could have been put together," she says incredulously, "but it has."

There is a sense of triumph when she recalls that period. She is excited as she explains, "I learned it is possible to build a dome by working with people like friends. It can be fun working. I never thought of work as fun before. But you really get something out of it."

Her family has been very survival-conscious. Her father, with a large family to support, had learned that it is difficult for a black man to survive and succeed in the atmosphere of the South. In New York, Mr. Fulton had obtained a position at Rockefeller University caring for the animals used in experiments. He had encouraged his children to get as much education as they could to compete in our economic system. That is why Roberta is so concerned about graduating from Seward High and finding a job as an assistant buyer in a department store.

Her association with CHARAS has given her an even wider perspective. "The guys at CHARAS look at the world and see one big family. Like, they'll do something for you without looking for a reward." Roberta laughs and relates that this is a very new attitude for her.

What seems to delight and confound her is finding other minority groups who are involved with people and not racing toward monetary goals. Although she's not always sure of what CHARAS is doing or why, she knows that the young men at the loft are different from the usual guys she meets. Trying to sum up her feeling, Roberta says, "The loft, like up there it's just home. I feel at home, just like in my own home. Even if we just sit around and watch TV, I like it. And the next time they build a dome, I want to be there."

When she is reminded of the sumptuous dinner she prepared with her friend Matty Small at the end of the first night's work on the dome (feeding over twenty people who had spent twelve hours working in the cold), she smiles. Her laughter is soft and her eyes have a charming quiet. With a new awareness, Roberta says, "You do it because you want to. That's the difference."

Tony Guitard

"You know, like too many people have too many problems, man. I want us not to have no problems. That's all." Tony has simple beliefs and needs. He has had little formal education and is not very articulate. But he desires a goodness in his life and the lives around him. Without any intellectual rationalizations, Tony has become sensitive to the excesses of our consumer society and its problems. A bitter smile crosses Tony's face as he thinks. Then, slowly, his words come as he looks shyly at you. "There should be a change, like for the future, you know, man. There are too many people who don' know wha's goin' on. They think tha' life is jes' goin' to work an' comin' back home. Tha's it. They hung up on material thin's of life."

A soft laugh escapes as he stretches his body from the tight cramped posture. He now relaxes and uses the back of the chair as a brace for his arching torso. He falls into a comfortable position and smiles again. "Like, man, sometimes I star' thinkin' what life's really all about, you know..." His voice trails off.

Tony Guitard was born in Puerto Rico, brought up in the South Bronx and for the last 4 years, has considered the CHARAS workshop his second home. He met Roy Battiste in the early 60s when both lived on the same block in the Bronx. Roy "hung out" with the other guys but was soon recognized as someone with aspirations that were different from most of the others. Roy was working for IBM at that time. But it was the things Roy was saying rather than the job he held that made the guys respect him. Tony would listen, often not fully aware of the significance of what he was hearing.

Roy's words sparked feelings Tony had but could not fully articulate. When Roy became fully involved with CHARAS, Tony came down to just hang out. He soon became infected with the sense of purpose and concern around him. He began to realize that many of the feelings and thoughts he had concerning how people could relate to one another were being practiced at CHARAS.

Tony had great respect for Roy. "You know, we all stood close." Tony reminisced as he sat at the kitchen table at the CHARAS workshop. "But Roy was someone I could look up to, you know, talk to when I had problems or whatever. Tha' help me a lot. Now I do for him wha' I can. Man, like he's gone through a whole lot of numbers. He didn' get any lucky breaks. He fought for it cause I 'member many days that the guys here, they had almos' nothin' to eat at all. But they kep' workin' at it. Other people, you know, they're thinkin' more about makin' it in the System. But Roy and these guys say 'later for this' and keep on going to their goal. I know people who would jes' cut loose from it and say 'fuck it.' But they stick to it."

Tony now looks regretful at what he's about to say. He would rather have it otherwise. But, he says, "man, like I know myself, I'm no leader. I'm more a follower, it may sound kinda funny, but I wan' America to jes' have peace of mind, you now. There too many things happenin' for a human bein' to jes' relax and stop to think. Tha's wha' the guys here in CHARAS try to do. Tha's why I come aroun'. Makes you feel like there's more to life, you know, then jes' 'makin' it.' An' tha's O.K., you know."

69

Luis Antonio Lopez

Luis was born twenty-two years ago in Cayey, Peurto Rico. By the time he was twelve, he was on his own. There was an abandoned U.S. Army base in his small town that the local YMCA had taken over. This Y became Luis' new home. It was there that he first experienced the feelings of community. This feeling remains with him today. Another experience that was to have a lasting effect was his meeting with Chino Garcia.

In 1967 Chino was spending a month in Puerto Rico making an evaluation of the Cayey YMCA program for the OEO office in Washington, D.C. Chino had made many interesting and important contacts in Washington who occasionally asked him to inspect or evaluate programs sponsored by OEO involving teen-age activities or facilities.

The conversations between Chino and Luis were long and inspiring. Luis was hearing of activities and programs that stimulated his own feelings of community. Luis' eagerness and energy so impressed Chino that he invited Luis to join him whenever he came to New York City.

After a short stint at the University of Puerto Rico (where he was active in college political life) and a hitch in the U.S. Navy, Luis came directly to New York City and moved in with Chino on the Lower East Side. He immediately became involved with the life and activities of CHARAS that were then in full swing. In this 69–70 period, Luis began working with Roy and Michael, studying dome-building principles. The idea of using domes as low-cost housing excited Luis' imagination.

Luis soon moved into the loft on Cherry Street. He and Roy began trying to make this deserted space habitable. There were constant battles with insufficient heat and boiler breakdowns. There was no hot water except that which they heated on the hot plate. Bathing facilities did not exist. An improvised kitchen had to be installed. But despite all the hardships and inconveniences, Luis and Roy created a living environment for themselves.

To divide space into various living quarters and open work areas, they decided to design and erect two domes made from canvas duck and two-by-fours. They were truly living the Fuller dictum "More with Less." Both domes cost under $50.00 and created a unique and exciting interior spatial feeling. The loft had finally assumed an atmosphere that was comfortable and representative of their principles.

Since involvement with CHARAS did not offer any salary, Luis was soon looking for employment. After a succession of jobs, he became the equipment coordinator for the School of Communications at Columbia University. He is responsible for the maintenance and scheduling of all audio-visual equipment used by the students in the department. Happily, his current interest in photography and his job coincide. He has an opportunity to investigate film techniques and equipment. His job offers him a range of experience and skills that he could manage no other way. It is the mastery of these skills that he wants to bring back to his community, through extended use of audio-visual techniques in documentation and teaching. Again, the community is important.

Luis, who is tall and lean, radiates a sense of assurance. He speaks with a deliberateness that denotes thoughtfulness. When he moves, the litheness of a gymnast attracts your attention. His whole being exudes a confidence that makes his thoughts appealing to any listener. He wants to communicate. When asked what he has learned from his two years with CHARAS, he states openly, "Well, I came to see that things I did before, like going to demonstrations and screaming, did nothing concrete. Here I find I am working with something that is very important—housing. That is one of the main problems we have. When I started to realize that people pay $25,000 to $35,000 for a house and only a quarter of it goes into actual building, I got angry. The other three-quarters goes into bureaucratic nonsense like insurance, overhead, profit, etc. A lot of people cannot afford housing like that. We can produce a dome plan that people could build themselves. That's why I'm with CHARAS. It makes me happy to think that those who have been excluded from proper housing because they are Puerto Rican, black or just poor and uneducated, now have a chance. If they can get out of the bullshit conditions existing now, get land to build on, then everybody has the potential for good housing and a better life. I'm not saying it's easy. It's not been for us. But we're sticking to it. Some of the early members have fallen away for many reasons. There was power-tripping going on by several. Others got into very heavy personal family responsibilities. But, so far, CHARAS is going on. Once we finish with this project, we won't have any money. But we'll go on. We'll knock on all the doors for the money we need for the future. Even if we don't get the money, we'll still try to continue. I learned how to build a dome, you know, how to go through the whole process. I could sit down and with just a little bit of multiplication and division and other mathematics, I could come out with a design for a house that I can build. It's so simple and practical. I really want other people to have that sense of accomplishment and joy. I want them to have the ability to build their own home and work with others who want the same. Sure many people say we work in our own ways. That we don't push hard enough. But, you have to remember, man, most of us come out of different backgrounds.

"We're not all accustomed to consistent pressure. That was one of the problems Michael had with us. He came from a middle-class mentality. When we were working on the Ruppert site dome, I had to cool Michael. He wants you to work hard all the time. I think this is good but you don't have to break your back. Well, we learned from each other. Michael would get annoyed at the apathy he first found when he started working with CHARAS. He wanted to teach us what he knew. He became impatient. But we had to learn how to become less apathetic and he had to learn to groove with people more. Now we have the same problem with the community. We want the community to be less apathetic about their conditions. We want them more involved. But it's tough. Having the dome out on Jefferson Street can help. It'll be something that the people can relate to directly. They will be able to see it, touch it and know that just people did it. People are tired of being told what's happening to them. That the city is fucked up. Nothing concrete really takes place. We try to talk less and just do our thing. We're not fantastic people, you know. We just learned that it could be done. And we're doing it. Our example might shake some of the apathy from the community. Who knows? But we're going to continue, or try to continue, and do what we have to do. Maybe, some of the people will catch the spirit and join us or do their own thing their own way. Great. We don't say we're the leader. We know the way is to try to get everyone to deal with their power trips and join forces together. We want everyone to work together. I don't know how it's going to work out. But I know none of us are going to be the same because of what happened to us here at CHARAS."

Felix Almodova

He works as a milkman now. He's up when the sun is just rising. There was a time when to be up that early meant Felix Almodova was out searching for a fix. Those days are long past. It was not easy. It took sixty days in jail to help him straighten his head. For the first time in his life, Felix began to seriously question what he was doing, why he was doing it, and the consequences of his actions. It all added up to a radical change. Four years of dope had twisted his life. He now had to rediscover himself.

Today, at twenty-four, Felix has been leading a new life. He works steadily. He and his wife, Terry, (once also addicted) are making their marriage succeed. He is going to night school to complete his high school education and is looking forward to enrolling in college. He sees the possibility of a writing career in his future. He also volunteers his time to CHARAS.

His small, wiry frame has the quality of a finely tuned watch spring. It takes time for Felix to look you in the eye. When he does, his eyes keenly fix themselves on you. His manner is diffident at times. This may be the result of being the third oldest of nine children. His father, a merchant seaman, was away most of the time. This made Felix the head of the family at a very early age. By the time he was eleven, Felix was helping support his family. He was born in the South Bronx and remained in the area through his late teen years. His mother and father liked to assume middle-class attitudes. Economically, though, the family existence hovered at the poverty level. This dichotomy created great confusion: he had to work to support his family yet could not get the fancy outfits his friends were sporting. Anger and disappointment were common to Felix during those days.

The South Bronx, in Felix's youth, had not yet become the seething ghetto it is now. "I saw the place change. I witnessed it," Felix recalls. "When I first grew up, the neighborhood was clean. My first recollections were of German and Jewish people in my area. There was also a large Irish population in the area. When I was young, I felt that I was into this 'I am an American' thing. But I ran into conflict when I came into contact with my own culture. As the neighborhood began absorbing more Puerto Ricans and blacks, my parents wouldn't let me hang out with them. I didn't understand it at all. And they used to rap Puerto Ricans. They were Puerto Ricans themselves. Sure my mother had proper schooling, as had my father. But they were into the whole middle-class trip while living a poor life."

Felix quickly relates how well he did until his sophomore year at high school. This was when he started hitting the street. "There was a big crowd, you know. We didn't joke a lot. We thought conservatively.

Very little horseplay. We tried to act like middle-class Puerto Ricans."
Felix laughs at this period of his life and the paradoxes it presented.
He remembers the time at junior high school when his depression
was fairly constant. "I was very poor. As an example, I couldn't get the
senior outfit. The other kids ridiculed me. And then in high school, I
was always the smallest. I always felt I was being picked on. It was
then I began smoking grass." Felix soon moved on to heroin.

At sixteen, he was working as an assistant on a milk truck. He
then quit school and enrolled in a city summer program to learn basic
gardening. He qualified as a Housing Authority gardener. But most
of his money, if not all, was soon spent on his habit. He was fiercely
determined that his mother not seek welfare. Felix's face grimaces
as he remembers. "I was ashamed of welfare. I didn't want none of
my friends to know I was ever on welfare. So I worked. But I didn't like
it because half my pay used to go to my mother. Then some friend
offered me some dope. And that was it. That took away four years, the
whole trip." When Felix finally was sent away for criminal trespass and
possession of stolen goods, he began his awakening process.

After getting out of prison, he met his future wife, who lived in
his neighborhood. Felix became the positive force in helping Terry
overcome her recently acquired habit. They became each other's rein-
forcement. Felix believes it was their power of love that helped them
through this difficult period.

At Thanksgiving, 1972, they were married. They told no one,
knowing the negative attitudes of Terry's family. Recalling the
troubles of that period, Felix can only concentrate upon the positive feelings and circumstances. "Happily," he says, "we had an
apartment. We have everything together. It was real cool. We had
everything worked out and it worked."

Felix had known Wilfredo Lopez from the first grade in school.
Everyone called Wilfredo "Beaver." No one could remember why. "He
was the first dude I knew," Felix proudly states. "We identified in a lot
of ways. Both of us were short. That helped us getting along so well.
We hung out a long time." During the time that Felix was getting married and restructuring his life, Beaver had begun to work and live at the
CHARAS loft. "It was in 72," recalls Felix, "Beaver told me what he was
into. I quickly became interested in domes. More important, I dug what
was happening around these people. I found people who were not afraid
to love each other as people. And that's spiritually healthy. It's also
healthy to do something voluntarily. Other people always want something for something, if you know what I mean. CHARAS wants nothing
from me. I like that. It's like meat I eat. I can sink my teeth into it."

Despite his schedule of working on the milk truck in the early morning, night school, sustaining his marriage to Terry, and continuing his relationship with his large family, Felix created time to spend with his new friends at CHARAS. He began learning the dome mathematics. He became fascinated with the simplicity of the structure. Michael Ben-Eli acted as the group's teacher. In Michael he discovered "a driving man." Felix also developed deep respect for Roy's determination. The entire situation became very inspirational. It all fit with a new image Felix had of himself. The reflection was pleasing and satisfying.

There is a deep philosophical strain in Felix. This becomes evident when he reviews his interrelations with CHARAS. His bright black eyes sparkle with the truth of inner revelation as he says, "It's hard to trust people. The things that are jumping off today, man. It's hard to trust anybody. There is a fear of being used. Also, there are a lot of people who are uptight. That used to get me depressed. I don't find much of any of this bullshit with the guys downtown. Sure, they have their own patterns. But they are willing to confront whatever it is. No holding back you know what I mean?"

Felix is very conscious of his own growth and development. He readily admits he's in an active transitional stage. "I'm rehabilitating myself," he says, with a sense of deep personal pride. "I got a lot of highway to go. I'm only now finding out about myself, really. When I feel like digging up an answer, I'll dig it up. But, now I see people, like in CHARAS, getting down with themselves. That's what I like. I don't like people shitting themselves. Those that do in life, do themselves in. If anyone at CHARAS gets that way, they will fail and leave or the whole group will die. I hope they don't. But, then again, you have to be real and admit it could happen."

Despite the occasional despair Felix may feel, he is generally positive about his future. "If I ever get into writing, I'll have a lot to say. I had problems, sure. But I'm looking for answers all the time. That's what I'll write about. Finding answers. And once I really find the answers, then I'll have to find the way to say it right. That'll be the test. But that's also the challenge."

It's probably this desire to search and define terms that Felix finds attractive in CHARAS. As long as this situation remains viable, Felix can be depended upon to volunteer his time. If Felix no longer discovers what he is seeking in CHARAS, he will search elsewhere. But, nonetheless, Felix is continuing with the search.

David Lorenzano

1971 was an important year for David Lorenzano. He had returned to New York from five months in Puerto Rico where he had been working at his uncle's slaughterhouse. Just prior to this, David had been court-martialed from the Marine Corps for being AWOL. This cost him five months in a Marine brig before he received an honorable discharge.

It was in 1971 that David also renewed his friendship with James Echevarria. They had grown up in the same South Bronx neighborhood. James, now involved with CHARAS, invited David to visit the loft on Cherry Street. David became quickly oriented to the CHARAS idea of researching means of developing low-cost housing and new life relationships. More important to David, he saw people working together in a way he never imagined possible. There was a spirit of community which he had sought in the Marines. That turned sour. But this feeling was true. Within a year, David was living at the loft. He shared duties, expenses and activities with Roy, Luis Lopez and whoever happened to need short or long term "crash" facilities.

David is nearly six feet tall, with the physique of an ex-Marine but the manner of one who is very conscious of his actions. He has dark wavy hair and warm brown eyes. He got his training as a printer while AWOL from the Marines. He had come to New York City and had hung out for a while. He then decided to learn printing, to get married and then not to, and to go back and face the Marine charges. After his discharge, David first worked as a printer, and then as an assistant in a bridal gown showroom. But it was at CHARAS that he began to know what he wanted to do and how to go about doing it.

It was at CHARAS that David was informed of a position at the Children's Art Workshop on East 6th Street. They were looking for an assistant to set up a printing shop to be used by the young participants of the Workshop and by the Lower East Side community organizations and individuals. He had the right background and, most important, a new perspective on community-oriented activities he had learned at the loft on Cherry Street.

In the basement of the Children's Art Workshop, David moves about with the confidence of a man in his own domain. Up above is the photo workshop and general meeting room. The sound of happily involved children echoes through the two levels of the Workshop. The basement space contains the graphics workshop and the printing facilities.

David's bearded face resembles that of the classic Roman athlete. His eyes have the same concentration as he carefully performs his printing chores. He looks up and flashes an inviting smile. "I got my own apartment up in the Bronx now." There is pride in this achievement. He is doing a job well, receiving money he feels happy earning, and fulfilling a responsibility that is meaningful to him. "Last summer I stayed at the loft for about four months. This year I had been living there for about five months. But now I got my own place. I dug living at the loft. We shared responsibilities on a communal level. Like, there were a few people living at the loft. Everybody just contributed to the loft. The bills were paid from those funds and food was bought. And everybody sort of survived from the contributions we made. If you were working and had money, you shared it. But even if you weren't working, you were helping to build domes without getting paid. It was an all-volunteer thing. People would work eight or nine hours, a day of hard labor, and not get paid. It was knowing you would get fed and sheltered that made contributing your time possible."

As David talks, he moves easily from the photo offset printer and plate washing table to the printing press, checking paper and ink and, finally, inspecting the finished product during a test run. He looks back smiling. The job has been done well. His feeling of achievement and accomplishment is again satisfied.

"When I think of CHARAS, I remember an attitude that was there and is still operating. The attitude is people doing what they really believe they want to do. Like, when Roy was teaching me what he knew of geodesic mathematics. He really wanted to teach me and I really wanted to learn. Not like when I was in school." David laughs meaningfully as he recounts this experience. His face now becomes transformed by a glowingly warm look of contentment as he goes on, "And like when we had finished this dome. We felt good. And, I didn't believe it would ever happen. I had the honor of meeting Bucky when he came down to look at the finished work. That was nice. But the idea of doing something you accomplished that can be of benefit to somebody, that was what was so terrific. Man, it made you feel good inside. Like I had never felt that way before. I feel the same way about what I'm doing here at the Workshop."

He looks around the room at eagerly absorbed young people working at their projects. "Guess it's really the same thing," David muses in a voice rich with satisfaction, "here or at CHARAS. When you do what you want to do, you do it willingly without any pushing from outside. What we have to do is to get more people into things where they work not only for bread but for what they enjoy or feel is important. Society will have to change. People can't go on just working at stupid jobs. I did for a while and really got fucked up."

David recalled the long cold days working on the dome as an expression of willingness overcoming hardships. "We spent eight to twelve hours working and there was no bitching. There was even a feeling of humor and warm vibes between people. There was a job to be done and an obligation to be fulfilled. We have learned it's a responsibility to give more support to each other to keep the CHARAS concept alive."

David stops his work for a moment and looks very intently off into space, trying to pull a thought from deep within him. He focuses and proceeds very seriously. "Our people have come from very heavy backgrounds, at least most of them. They have become more open-minded people. They don't let their hang-ups intervene with their relationships with other people. So, we hang in better, maybe, than a lot of other people who are out to just get a quick buck. If you've been strung out or been in prison, you begin to realize, or at least we have, that there has to be more than just hustling out on the street. You want to reach up to something better for you and everyone. You know, you don't fuck-up by yourself. Everything around you either helps you do one thing or another. When I was growing up in the South Bronx, near everyone was getting into drugs in a heavy way. I stayed clear. I didn't like what I saw some of my friends become. I hung out on the street, sure. But I went to centers and played a lot of basketball. And my family didn't hassle me too much. They made me feel all right and that was good." David now looks relaxed and continues his work routines.

He suddenly laughs again as he says, "Before coming down to CHARAS, I had a different outlook on life. My eyes are now open to reality. I used to think that everything was just happiness, hanging out at parties, things like that. Now I realize that a simple thing like housing can help the oppression people live with. It has been a great thing to understand. This new reality has made me very aware of the changes needed for so many people. It changed my life because it opened my mind. Yeah, if I had been this aware before, maybe I'd never have gone AWOL or any of the other shit that happened in my life. Yeah, maybe, maybe everything would have been a little differ-ent." David nods his head in deep agreement with himself and goes off to put a finished plate onto the printing press. He soon loses him-self in the careful attention he is giving his work. As the paper begins to shoot out of the machine, he reviews the completed effort and smiles, looking pleased with his work.

Mark Spagnola

Just as Bucky Fuller tried over 50 years ago to unprogram himself from all that had been taught him, so, at twenty, Mark is involved with trying to unprogram all he has learned about himself, his relationship to art, the art scene and the world around him. There have been many conflicting influences in Mark's life. His early childhood was spent in the Greenwich Village area. When he was three, Mark's family moved to Union, New Jersey, then a very suburban environment. His summers were spent on his grandparents' farm in upper New York State. Throughout this entire period, he was constantly drawn back to New York and the people who made up the "street life" of the city.

His tall frame, black hair tied back into a pony-tail, large limpid dark eyes, his jeans and workshirt and his quiet voice that makes you lean closer to hear, give Mark the appearance and style of many of today's young people who are searching for their own truth and function. Nothing is accepted or taken for granted. Mark considers his present studies at the School of Visual Arts in Manhattan a journey of discovery and experience. He is not looking for a diploma to fit into any societal groove. Mark confides, "What do I think is valuable? Well, whether this country is going to be worth staying in, for one. I'm trying to make a decision whether I want to stay in this country or go to one of the countries that are going to be up and coming this century."

New systems and styles of existence are of interest to Mark. He is curious about the many different life influences exerted on art, the influence art may have on our lives. When he talks about art, he refers to it in structural terms. "People start looking in other areas. I see people looking into anthropology, ancient and present. They are looking at things structurally and tying in mathematics and other scientific things. They are interested in the whole structure; in the way things are put together."

In 1970, when the Environmental Communications Research Center was established at the School of Visual Arts, Mark enrolled. It was there he met Roy Battiste and others from CHARAS. Roy had been asked to build a geodesic dome and then he remained as an instructor for a short period. Mark recalls that the Center had twenty people who were called instructors and never more than fifty students. "We all worked together," Mark remembers. "It was rather loose. It eventually dissolved because of its own bureaucracy and hangups. But it was a good experience for everybody involved. I learned a lot from it."

Mark vividly remembers the cardboard dome that Roy and other CHARAS people built at the Center. He met Michael Ben-Eli when Michael gave several lectures there. He soon met friends of Roy's and

Michael's. Their involvement with Bucky Fuller led him to read Fuller's books and attend related seminars. Mark links all of this activity directly to his interest in art and society. "Let's get into the idea of the geodesic domes and sculpture. I thought it was really nice. I wanted to know where is it going from there? And then I started rapping about urban problems, bringing people out of the cities and creating low-cost housing." Mark was actively associating his art with the society around him. He found, in Roy and CHARAS, active resources for his inquiring mind. He would drop around once or twice a week to sit and rap.

The atmosphere at CHARAS pleased Mark immensely. He slowly became aware of the various problems CHARAS faced in its fight for existence. "I think they're doing a really together job. They're getting something done in an area where it's really hard. You always have to deal with city or state bureaucracy and money is a big hassle. But there's a good atmosphere because people down there are very loose and very friendly. It's a god way to work. And in its loose, informal manner, it's a learning experience for everybody."

Mark believes the strongest bond holding CHARAS together is friendship. "It's a whole group of friends working together, when they can. Roy, sort of, keeps things together. He knows an incredible amount of people. Some people you see down there, they're working just for a day or two. You don't see them for six months after that. But you know they're around. And each person has certain skills. When they're needed, they can be found. Sure, sometimes it gets hard to get things done because people are scattered, but that's the way it works."

Having rapport with street people, Mark understands their thinking. He realizes that many of the people who form CHARAS came from "street" orientations or are still very involved with the street life of hanging out, goofing and limited responsibility or awareness beyond the individual's need to survive. Yet he sees in CHARAS a new molding for these people. "Being mostly street people, they have gradually picked up on different things and gotten into them. But once they come to CHARAS, I don't know how much they remain street people any more except for the information of the street experience of hanging out with some friends."

Mark also values the respect that is shown for individual privacy. "I don't know the backgrounds of most of the people there. When we're working, doing things or hanging out, we just talk about things that people are into now. Whatever people's backgrounds are, well, it's behind them. Their background is just their experience. That is their particular way they learned to deal with people." He may have learned that, at times, it's best not to know. The "now" of someone's existence may be more important to understand and deal with than the "past."

Having lived part of his youth in the country, Mark also understands CHARAS' desire to find alternates to accepted city life patterns. "They're trying to break out of the city," Mark reflects. "The city is a maze and a prison to many people CHARAS knows. They want to be able to take a lot of people out of the maze." Mark's voice now becomes very soft as he says, "You know, there is a philosophy operating down there. They may not be aware of it, but it's there. And it's a very noble gesture, too. The philosophy, when it works is 'I learned this and I'll teach it to you.'" Mark likes to think he wants to live that way also.

In the time Mark has given serious thought to the interaction of technology and society, he has concluded that a tribal experience among people will have to develop with the increase of technology. "I think that the technological society and the tribal existence will have to merge together. You can't say that you can take this and combine it with that and come out with an idealistic situation because you're not dealing with an ideal situation. You're dealing with reality. And you keep your feet on the ground by doing things." That is probably the strongest reason why Mark hangs out at CHARAS. He believes they are doing things and doing them with a new vision.

David Latouche

David describes himself as a 26-year-old high school graduate, college dropout, itinerant carpenter and a Lower East Sider. This last statement of identity with a place is now a continuously occurring experience for him. His upbringing in comfortable Montclair, New Jersey had left strong evidences of alienation and personal dissatisfaction. It was not until he found his girl, Lynn Tiefenbacher, and the 6th Street Children's Art Workshop (which Lynn supervises) that the pieces began to fall into place.

With his pony-tailed blond hair and "granny" glasses, David Latouche resembles a pioneer of the late 1800s hewing a clearing for his farm. In fact, he uses his artistic talents and mechanical abilities to keep the Workshop operating. He has sunk roots in the community that has become home for him and feels the comfort of belonging. The living space he created from a tenement basement has an openness that reflects his sense of ease and assurance.

David has an incisive, stoic and probing attitude towards his reality. He faced many difficulties in his teen years trying to find a form for his aspirations in art. Sitting back in his kitchen chair, David ruefully recalls those days, the effort and anguish crossing his face as he speaks. "I used to write and I used to do cross-county running. Which was nice, too. But I guess since I was 15, I have been involved in terms of trying to actually create a new art form rather than just reading or looking at art stuff. It's a different way of doing it. By the way, I haven't written anything in years."

He gets up from the table to make some tea. He looks back at you, his eyes squint as he thinks, and then he begins working out his thoughts as he speaks. "It goes into terms of the total concept of what you're doing." His voice, soft and confident, still has traces of his suburban background—an accent foreign to the Lower East Side. Bringing his mug of tea to the table, he sits and stretches his work-booted legs out as far as they reach. His eyes capture you again as he goes on, "Like, if you're doing something, you can think of it in sculptural terms. You can think of it in visual terms of color, in terms of how it's going to affect what goes on around it. Some situations are more prosaic. You don't get all the glamour."

David recalls meeting Roy Battiste three years ago in a neighborhood photo shop. He was aware of the dome-building activities of CHARAS from articles in the *Whole Earth Catalog*. He immediately began dropping in at the 10th Street storefront CHARAS was then using. David had already read about dome mathematics. He questioned Ed Schlossberg (Bucky's assistant, who first worked with the CHARAS group) about equations that bothered him. He indicated his interest in helping whenever any building would take place.

Thereafter, his contact was more as a friend to Roy and the others. Whenever David heard that an extra hand was needed or his VW van could be of use, he would appear to offer his services. The way in which word circulated that help was needed was never direct or specific. There was a pioneer spirit of knowing your neighbor needed help and you appeared and volunteered whatever was needed. This sense of community is very strong among many of the Lower East Side. It gave David a sense of comfort, knowing he was part of it.

When the 5.6 inches of rain hit New York City, threatening the two domes erected by CHARAS, David and his friend Christopher Miller rode up to the building site and began to help with the task of preserving the dome. David simply knew that Roy would be in trouble and short-handed. He was close by and available. For five very long and wet hours he toiled with the others to save the domes from the hard rains. The feeling of community and neighborliness was acted out again.

Several weeks later, the final stage of the dome-building cementing was to take place early on a Saturday morning. David, Lynn and Christopher were on hand to help. The way so many people came to work was reminiscent of bygone barn-raisings. The work was arduous and the weather cold yet a festive feeling of celebration pervaded the atmosphere. It may be this spirit of cooperation and concern that prompted David to observe stoically, "CHARAS' going along with it and they're dealing with it. They have their ups and they have their downs. It's all part of the same thing. And they will get there."

Matty Small

Matty Small has been slowly expanding her horizons. From the time she was four and her family moved into the LaGuardia Project until very recently, her boundaries were limited to her immediate neighborhood. She went to local elementary and junior high schools. Her high school was a short bus ride away. She then worked for two years in a nondescript job for the telephone company on 14th Street. She is now enrolled in the Bronx Community College Nursing Program. This is the farthest Matty has physically travelled from her neighborhood. But the spiritual focus of her existence centers on the project building on the Lower East Side.

In September, 1972, Matty first met the young men who frequented the loft building at 303 Cherry Street. They called themselves members of CHARAS. It was Matty's first significant encounter with young people whose outlook and aspirations demanded considerable thought from her. Her other friends didn't require any intellectual or spiritual adjustments. These newly acquired friends did.

Matty was seated with her friend Roberta on the benches outside her project building. Roberta is small and girlish in appearance while Matty has the fullness and voluptuousness of a woman far beyond her twenty-one years. Her dark skin glistened, absorbing the warm sunlight. In the idle banter between these young women, Matty's voice had a vibrant timbre of assurance.

Sitting there in the early March sun, they laughed readily at each other's stories and comments. Matty was reminding Roberta of her first series of meetings with the CHARAS group, especially with James and Roy. "Meeting them, through you, sure that was something else. I mean, you meet them, and you find that they're great people." Roberta laughed her infectiously rich laugh. "Yeah," Roberta speaks through her laughter, "you still had your kid scardiness about those buildings across the street." Matty fully agreed. "That's right. We kids used to call that place 'the warehouse factory' and were really scared to go in. Like the first time I went into the building with you, I kinda got the chills. It was a creepy place."

Roberta begins a low chuckle. She points to the third floor of the warehouse building across the street. "And when you walked in, girl, you looked around and said, 'Hey, this is fantastic.'" "That's right." Matty cuts in quickly. "You know, the way they put up the sections and built things, I thought it was great. It was a great job. A lot of people build things but they had the paintings and everything when you first come in." Her glowing smile was enraptured. Matty was again reliving the excitement of that first entrance to the loft space. Breathlessly, she went on, "It looked like a good place for a person to stay." Matty now became giggly. "You know, Roberta, I wouldn't mind living in a place like that, to be honest with you."

Well, I told you you'd like the place and the guys," Roberta gleefully bubbled on. "Like you've told me so many times before, most of the people around here, you meet them and say hi! and that's about it. They don't know how to talk."

Matty readily agreed. "But the people in the loft, they start talking to you like they've known you for years. They really know how to come out and talk to you. It's not like so many of the guys in the projects who say hi! and that's it, I have no more to say to you, I don't know where you're coming from." Matty and Roberta exchanged knowing looks concerning the encounters they have had. "But those guys, they talk to you and try to find out where you're coming from, what you're like," Matty continued. "This way, they could talk to you better because they know where you're coming from. They make you feel at home in everything."

Roberta has lit a cigarette and offers one to Matty who lights it, draws in the smoke and exhales quickly as she has another thought she wants to communicate to Roberta. "You can't meet them and say Boy! I don't dig this one right off the bat because you get talking to them for quite a period of time. You know something," Matty says vehemently to Roberta, "I haven't met anyone that said they didn't like the people from the loft. I think they're just fantastic, really."

Whenever free, together or singly, Matty and Roberta would go up to the loft to help with any of the preliminary work during the preparation of the cardboard sections for the future domes. They would contribute their efforts openly and without fear of being rejected because of machismo attitudes. This pleased them. They had never worked with tools before but were eager to learn and to do whatever they could. As Matty enthusiastically says to Roberta, "The people there jst want to get together to build domes and I thought that it was really great that they want to build something that people could learn to live in in future years. I enjoyed every minute helping them."

Their conversation has now turned to clothes shopping they are planning during the next days.

The idea of domes and related technical matters is still baffling to them and their future involvement with CHARAS may be limited, but they have experienced an alternate set of values that will sustain them.

Wilfredo Lopez

Wilfredo Lopez is called "Beaver" by everyone who knows him well. He does not remember how or when this nickname began. But Beaver is his name. He will soon graduate from Long Island University as a sociology major, if he sticks it out. During the summer of 73, Beaver had a job in a new Board of Education after-school teen-age activity program on West End Avenue in Manhattan. Nothing unusual so far.

But Beaver came out of the gloom of the South Bronx where he spent his youth living in an Eagle Avenue low-income housing project. As he was growing up, the gangs were breaking up and drugs were taking over. At present, the gangs are back again.

His father died in 1961 when Beaver was twelve. Mr. Lopez owned a grocery store in the Bronx which occupied his full attention. Although it was the center of his life, Mr. Lopez barely saw any profit from this small establishment. In actuality, Beaver sadly admits, the store drained his father. This hard-working man found it difficult to relate to his wife and children. Soon after the father's death, Beaver's older brother Carlos sought his escape through drugs. Another brother, Luis, was fourteen (three years younger than Carlos) and soon followed Carlos into the drug subculture. An older brother and sister were away caring for their own families. Beaver, except for his friend Felix Almodova, was alone.

It was not until 1965 that the two brothers began breaking the grip of addiction. They joined a Synanon drug rehabilitation community and began to move away from the horror and indignity of the junkie world. During those four years, Beaver attempted to withdraw from the family chaos and alienation. He developed sensitive behavior patterns. Although he "hung out" with the project youth of his age, he was not overly gregarious and had a strong need for privacy in his social engagements.

In a rare comment about himself, Beaver stated, "I learned the hard facts of reality early in my life." His real education was gained watching his two junkie brothers and the street life of the Eagle Avenue area. Yet he did well at school and enjoyed the academic and athletic achievements he discovered there.

During this period in Beaver's life, while in junior high school, his gym teacher, Mr. Korowitz, encouraged him to perfect his talent for gymnastic sports. Mr. Korowitz saw promising athletic potential in Beaver's small and agile body. Also a coach of New York University's swimming team, he wanted Beaver's eventual participation in the team. While at DeWitt Clinton High School, Beaver was brought to the attention of athletic scouts for Morehouse College in Atlanta, Georgia. Beaver had, somehow, expected to go on to NYU but he had learned to be a pragmatist on the Bronx streets. He had learned not to live on promises but on that which was immediately obtainable.

Morehouse College had had Martin Luther King as a distinguished graduate. A very respected black college, Morehouse wanted to attract other minority students. That was why Beaver, in 1967, accepted a scholarship to Morehouse, to Mr. Korowitz's great regret.

Morehouse College was a strange and disquieting experience for Beaver. He was one of only five Puerto Rican students. He was, also, a light-skinned Puerto Rican. But it was not these distinctions that upset Beaver.

In his early Eagle Avenue and school experiences, the blacks he knew were similar to him in outlook. A basic philosophy of "don't let the 'man' get you down" and "beat the system any way you can" was the pervasive attitude of most of the blacks and Puerto Ricans he had known.

At Morehouse he discovered a highly motivated black student population. They had very strong middle-class objectives regardless of their backgrounds. Many of these black students did not have the scars of city ghetto life. To Beaver, these young men and women were a whole new breed. He had difficulty assimilating their standards or aspirations. This adjustment proved so disturbing and confusing that he had to reassess and review major beliefs he had held his entire life. Within two months after arriving, Beaver returned to New York City feeling the immense pressure of deep personal upheaval and uneasiness.

After some time of deep reflection, Beaver decided to enroll at Long Island University, in Brooklyn, as a sociology major commencing September, 1968. He had applied for and received sufficient student loans that made him independent of family support. During the early part of the first semester at LIU, Beaver married a young woman from his old neighborhood. The new financial demands necessitated dropping out of college. Beaver found a job at the post office. He was able to pick up his college career a short time thereafter while still working at the post office. But the stresses at this time were extreme. The attempt to establish his marriage and the pressures of work and college had their eroding effect. By 1970, Beaver and his wife separated.

At about this same time, Jose Sosa, a college friend, had introduced him to Roy Battiste. Roy was seeking workers for a forthcoming CHARAS summer program sponsored by the Neighborhood Youth Corps. Roy wanted to teach basic dome-building principles to these workers so that they could, in turn, train some Lower East Side kids. Jose and Beaver accepted the job and spent the summer of 1970 working in the CHARAS program.

Beaver became very involved with the program. He also became concerned with the community orientation of CHARAS as an organization. Basically a loner, he was now learning the joys of participation and mutual attainment of goals. His interest and association with CHARAS was finally capped in the winter of 1972, when Beaver moved into the loft at Cherry Street, sharing it with Roy and a friend, Luis Lopez.

Despite the hardships under which they lived (no hot water or bathing facilities and infrequent heat in winter), a new triad of leaders was being formed with Beaver, Luis and Roy. The sense of "community" grew among these three and those whom they attracted to the loft. There was strong motivation and direction evident. For the first time, a sense of purpose occupied Beaver's activities.

The next year flowed for Beaver. There was the intensity of work towards building the projected domes. But soon a basic conflict developed—his newly awakened social awareness made him uncomfortable with the passive attitude CHARAS had toward overt social trends or conditions. Beaver wanted CHARAS to become involved in more dynamic socially activated programs beyond the planning and building of domes. Also, a new relationship with a quiet and lovely young Puerto Rican woman, Niki, created a need for greater privacy. He and Niki were attempting to develop a personal relationship in an atmosphere geared to communal existence rather than private convenience. An inevitable schism grew. With it came an uneasiness between Beaver and the two others living at the loft.

During the September, 1972 to January, 1973 building period, Beaver worked as energetically as he could alongside the regulars and vast number of occasional people who came and went. But very soon after the dome was completed, he and Niki moved out of the loft and, maybe, out of the aura of CHARAS.

There may have been too many conflicted areas within Beaver for him to successfully devote himself to CHARAS or any other similar organization. But, whatever the future holds for Beaver, a memory of some very good times will remain with him.

The Guide and Friend

Michael Ben-Eli

Upon first meeting Michael, you are struck immediately by a tall, boy-ishly handsome young man with a ready smile and outgoing quality. Further contact reveals deeper aspects—intelligence, meticulous-ness, grasp of overall problems, and the means to resolve complex questions. Michael emerges as an exceptional person you know will continue to grow and develop.

He was born twenty-nine years ago in Israel to pioneer parents. That spirit of individualism combined with a strong concern for those around him is still very much part of Michael. His mother, from Spanish and Italian backgrounds, brought a fine sense of the arts to her new homeland. Michael's father came penniless from Russia, burning with zeal. As founder and director of Israel's first maritime museum, Arie Ben-Eli still has the same energy that carried him through the 48 war and the enormous struggle to create the museum.

It is this heritage that fed Michael during his formative years. When Michael was five, his father, somehow, took Michael along on patrols into the hostile desert. Michael began to quickly learn the techniques of keen awareness and survival. During summer vacations, he went with his father on deep-sea expeditions seeking lost maritime trea-sures. The specifics of scientific detail began to fascinate him. Later, Michael would spend long afternoons at the museum studying the antique maps, coins, and seacraft paraphernalia. His imagination was ripe with the wonder of ancient mariners and their skills. This absorp-tion of information and ideas was more beneficial than the formal schooling he was receiving. Michael did not like the rigid demands and control of his classes. Only strong parental intervention prevented him from dropping out of school.

Near the end of his high school education, Michael decided that architecture was to be his future field of study. He also felt that the traditional schooling available in Israel was not for him. He needed freedom, exploration and discovery to feed his fertile mind. He was to have two and one half years to resolve this problem as a 2nd Lieutenant in the Israeli Army. This period was a calming pause for him. There was little if any hostility at this time. Therefore, Michael had long days and nights to think and re-think all that had occurred to him. Strangely, the discipline of army life began to give Michael the inner control he had not previously developed. He was released at the age of 21 and immediately left for England.

Two of Michael's friends, also interested in architecture, had heard about a school in London and had discussed it with Michael. It was not really a school as they had known it. It was founded in the nine-teenth century by a group of young men who were strongly against traditional university education. They set about organizing a school of architecture with teachers who were practicing architects. Thus the attitudes and educational climate of the school depended upon who happened to be teaching and their interaction with students. This was the basic atmosphere of the Architectural Association as Michael encountered it in 1964.

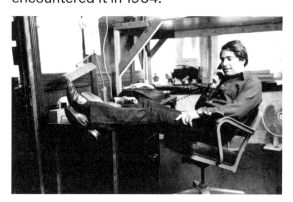

Many students float and dissipate time in an open situation like A.A. The discipline Michael learned while in the army helped him overcome this hazard. He dug in. Mathematics, which had been a hardship while in high school, now became a fascinating new discovery. Michael had truly begun to investigate his own potentials. He was finding this experience a vital and stimulating exercise in his educational development.

Michael, during the first year at A.A., acquired a learning pattern that he now uses constantly. He found that most scientific subjects are taught as if they are inherently difficult. These classes are conducted by teachers who learned from secondary sources. Wherever possible, Michael attempted to go directly to the original source. In this manner the mystery of learning was eliminated. He was surprised to learn that those thinkers who were supposed to be the most difficult and incomprehensible were the sharpest, the clearest and the most beautiful. This experience taught him to make a rule of going straight to the source for his information and to nowhere else.

Toward the end of his first semester, Michael went to a lecture. What he heard completely altered the course of his life. The lecture was given by R. Buckminster Fuller.

Bucky had come to London in January, 1965 to address the British Architectural Students' Association. Bucky wanted architectural schools, all over the world, to conduct an integrated program of studying problems related to world resources and world needs. He then wanted "design solutions" to be proposed as answers to these questions. In 1965, few were concerned with world environment or pollution. Yet, Bucky realized the importance and the need of answers to these pressing issues.

Michael listened intently. He had come to the lecture only out of curiosity. Near the lecture's end, Michael turned to Keith Critchlow, a tutor at the A.A., and talked about how moved he was and how much he would like to help participate. Keith said that he had met Bucky the previous year. Through the British Architectural Association, Keith had also done some work with Bucky. And, by chance, Keith was going to have breakfast with Bucky the next morning. Keith inquired whether Michael would like to join them. Michael, enthusiastically, responded "Yes." At that breakfast meeting, Michael began his work relationship and friendship with Bucky. Michael was soon involved in helping plan and install a big exhibition in the Tuileries Gardens of Paris. The following year, Michael spent several months in Ghana, Africa. Here, Michael and Keith worked on design problems, trying to utilize native building materials in the construction of domes. With Bucky, they planned a large aluminum dome for lectures. It was built with the aid of students from the local university.

In 68, there was a major conference and exhibition of Bucky's works. Again, Michael was involved. The contact with Bucky, which began so casually in 1965, was now becoming more frequent and important. Bucky began to see he could rely on Michael. He also recognized Michael's ability to grasp the nuance of geodesic thinking and the emerging idea of Bucky's World Games technique of solving world problems. Briefly, World Games is an approach to studying the global needs of humanity and producing plans which can be initiated for the benefit of all mankind.

Michael's own work at A.A. began to center more and more on urban problems and means of resolving them. What was immediately apparent to him was the lack of any scientific approach to urban problems. He also discovered that the language used to discuss or describe urban problems was not concise or unified. Each expert was inventing his own terms. There was more development of a mystique than a desire to really solve problems.

At about this time Michael met Professor Gordon Pask of System Research, Ltd. Prof. Pask's organization is a non-profit group for research in cybernetics and behavioral sciences. Through Pask, Michael began his inquiry and interest in cybernetics and the study of joint systems. This new field of study fit in nicely with everything he had learned from Bucky. It was also possible to synthesize Bucky's ideas with Pask's concept of developing proper investigatory procedures and solutions.

By 1969, Bucky asked Michael to come to the United States and work with him at Carbondale, IL. There, at the University of Southern Illinois, Bucky had established his World Games headquarters. Michael did not have a chance to do any studying at Carbondale since most of his time was with Bucky. This meant following Bucky's incredible schedule of traveling from lecture to conference on a nearly constant basis.

At the many lectures and seminars Michael attended with Bucky during this period, Michael began to realize that the problem was not the technological and scientific potential but, rather, the lack of a purely organizational process, on global terms, of focusing and channeling this necessary work.

At about this time Gordon Pask was appointed Professor at Brunel University in London. Michael enrolled in the graduate program. He was going to try to create a system to help organize technological and scientific information and personnel for the benefits of all men. This would be his thesis. Maybe more, his life work. The year of 1970 was spent partly in London between his visits to New York City to continue the work he had begun with the CHARAS group.

Chino and Angelo had contacted Bucky in January of 1970. They represented a small group of Puerto Rican young men who seemed interested in building domes. It was their idea that, in time, they could develop their dome-building skills into a commercial activity. Bucky seemed impressed with their sincerity and asked Michael to spend some time with them. It was thought that Michael would work with them as he had worked with many college groups before. He would assist and supervise them in the erection of a dome and then move on. But was not the situation Michael encountered when he first visited the CHARAS group.

Michael recalled his feelings and memories of these initial meetings and further two years of work, struggle and success with CHARAS while seated in the 21st floor, Upper East Side, bright and modern apartment of his bride to be, Marcia McElrath. This comfortable apartment, with its paintings (by Marcia, who worked as Art Director for *World Magazine*), modern furnishings, airy view of New York was in vivid contradiction to the conditions he found while working and living with the CHARAS people.

Michael's usual expression of warmth and outgoing spirit becomes somewhat saddened as he thinks back to those early days. His look and voice develop a dull, listless quality. They convey the dismay and basic shock he experienced at his first sessions. "Most of them didn't have any orderly school education. They had no mathematical concepts in their backgrounds. I realized immediately they had no resources, no money, no place to work, really nothing."

Michael recalls that most of the guys were drinking a lot at that time and had poor attention spans and limited conversational potentials. "I realized to build a dome, or give them a blueprint of how to build one didn't make sense. What was really wanted was a training program. Basic knowledge. Then they would be able to understand what it is to really build a dome. So, I decided to start this program. Yah, it took about a year."

1970 was an extremely difficult year for Michael. That winter, Michael had very little money. He lived with the CHARAS group as best he could. Luckily, he was asked to teach at Columbia University that winter. That income was helpful in starting his project. Michael's entire body seems to wince, reliving those hard winter days. "We used to live in all kinds of cellars on the Lower East Side, all kinds of places. Sometimes we were frustrated by not being able to buy pencils and paper. It was also very difficult to interest people in supporting our program because there was nothing we could show."

The problems of that period were not only external but very strongly internal as well. "It was very difficult to hold their attention. They could not see what the connection was of all the things I was talking about, all the triangles and cosines, and the one thing they wanted to do. Namely, to build a house."

In this early period, there was a band of about seven that attended "classes" conducted by Michael. Due to the erratic schooling conditions, or lack of them, the people attending these sessions had great difficulty in comprehending the intangibles involved in dome mathematics and concepts. "They had been conditioned to see and understand their reality of immediate survival. It was very hard to see a few steps ahead. To some extent, this is still true when complex planning is needed. But they have certainly come a long way."

The degree of dissatisfaction and disillusionment during this early period was the worst Michael had ever experienced. His voice has the strain of not wanting to admit the depth of depression he had known then. He takes a long look out the window at the extended landscape of the city before he goes on. "It was very unsatisfying. You couldn't see any fruits of your labor. I really don't now what gave me the patience to go on. There was no feedback at all. It looked hopeless all the time. In fact, there were quite a few times I was at the point of giving it all up. Now, this is something I don't like to do in principle. That is probably why I continued. But, somehow, things grew. Roy became most secure with what I was doing. He had more background than the rest. It became easier for him to understand. And, through some friends by the end of that year, we managed to get the Container Corporation of America to produce the needed shell of the dome. It was going to be a new form of corrugated board they had developed from paper.

"Then in 1971, a grant from the New York State Council on the Arts came through. CHARAS was given $15,000 to research and build two domes on a site in the Lower East Side."

Michael now became very philosophical, reflecting retrospectively on that first year. He settles effortlessly into a leather Mies van der Rohe chair. He has given his thoughts consideration for some time. He now speaks freely and with ease. "I think that in life you have to be able to oscillate between freedom and structure and order. Freedom is probably the most difficult thing there is. You have to work very hard to build a freedom. A society truly built upon freedom can exist only after a structuring has taken place. It can be a very loose structuring, but it has to be structured. What I'm really talking about is the kind of free-dom only a master painter can achieve after 20 or 30 years of struggle. But, primarily you're talking about a process, a problem process, and a process that is organized because of background and training. In CHARAS you had little of this. You had a group of young men with really good vision who had undergone major changes in their con-ceptual orientation to life. They turned from things like mugging and other negative episodes to activities of great positive worth. But they had absolutely no ideas, no previous training, no tradition, nothing of knowing how to really change a concept into a reality. And they had a tendency, I think, to shy away from problems. In that case they were a little bit like children in their enthusiasms. When the task resisted, they would lose interest. I think that this is something which is pretty much a social-cultural privation. Any schooling, no matter how bad (and most today are bad), trains you to put a concentrated effort to break a problem. Most of the people in CHARAS never had this.

"I discovered the only way to overcome this tremendous gap was to have patience. The only way you can get a group like this to grow and develop is by deliberately creating situations that will be immediate and striking. Anybody involved will really understand what is right or wrong. You've got to bring forth spontaneous understanding. It's not a question of textbooks or authority.

"And it takes time. You have to wait before the realization dawns, is understood and is converted automatically to self-motivated knowledge.

"There were times I was depressed. I was very anxious. I tried to push them hard sometimes. Until I realized there's no question of pushing anybody, or telling them or shouting or anything like this. You have to have patience and see how it develops. And in a society where it is said that time is money, this kind of thinking is very difficult. But it is necessary. If we can get people, all people, to think then many of the problems will be understood and, maybe, solutions will be created.

"I really learned that from Bucky. I often heard him talk about sharing all you know. He looks at it as an absolutely matter of fact thing. He feels that it's almost your responsibility to share your knowledge and your advantage with other human beings.

"I also learned that nothing can be done in one day. And the one thing that overwhelmed me with CHARAS was just how long it took to get going. Yet, I think the results are very positive. But it took an incredible effort. Not physical effort. But of time. You have got to totally reorient your thinking about 'time is money.' But you must begin to count the incredible amount of results you can get by educating all people."

Michael's level of intensity and energy is extremely high now. He stands and looks about the long living room space. He has more work to do. He's about to tackle his first "commercial" job of originating and building a complex for an Israeli orange juice concern. He is eager to see if all that he has learned from Bucky and the men at CHARAS can somehow be utilized in this new venture.

He calls out for his "Miss Marcia" and says, "Let's eat." Michael walks towards the dining table with the assurance of knowing the food will be good and that tomorrow will, somehow, be met very surely and firmly. There is work to be done and Michael looks forward to it.

The Original Six

Chino Garcia

"Man what time is it," Chino mumbled as he opened the door. The tenement room was steaming and dark. The noisy fan did little but blow papers about on the folding-table-turned-desk. He had awoken from a restless sleep. He lumbered back to the couch and dropped down, exhausted, struggling to keep his crumbled boxer shorts from falling below his ample stomach.

When he was told it was 2 P.M., he forced himself up and staggered toward the kitchen sink, turning on the cold water. The apartment was three cramped rooms. It had a front living room which was crowded with furniture and cartons of books and papers; a rear, windowless bedroom with only a small cabinet toilet without sink or bath and a kitchen in the middle acting as an entrance hall with the classic covered bathtub serving as a counter. There wasn't any ventilation and the building's age showed on the walls and ceilings.

Chino Garcia and his wife, Ruth, live on 3rd Street in the heart of the once romantic "East Village" but really the Lower East Side. Chino was asleep so late in the afternoon because he had driven a taxi for a twelve-hour shift the previous night to augment his income from a community action group, NENA.

Chino, his fatigue obviously still engulfing him, rose from the couch and shuffled to the refrigerator, bringing out two cans of beer. Then sitting at the makeshift desk, he looked at the various piles of correspondence to and from city agencies, neighborhood action groups, and the like. He handed over one of the beers and a sheet of paper. "Do you dig what I've written?"

The paper contained three thick paragraphs outlining the purposes of his fellow participants in CHARAS for a funding application. He accepted the comment that the page was very clear and precise. "Great man, I sweated over that mother for two days. I sure hope they dig what we're doing and what we want to do." He took a long swig of beer from the can. "Those dudes at those foundations have to have some of their heads changed. We have to get into a rap with them. Share an exchange of heavy ideas." He sat back and smiled. That's what's beautiful about rapping. Fixes up your head." He quickly banged his head to emphasize his point. "Takes out the shit and puts in some new stuff." Again, he smiled and leaned in close. "Sometimes I think there's too much to think about. But that's what's so dynamite now." He laughed a satisfying laugh.

"Hey, let's sit out on the stoop. Too hot in here," Chino said as he pulled on his farmer coveralls and T-shirt. The mild April afternoon had brought the street alive with people and the sounds of traffic. There were many people strolling or lounging on other stoops. There was a group of men playing dominos sitting on milk crates and balancing the board on their knees. Others gathered in small knots of wives with children or men gossiping. The street suddenly seems to bloom when the weather is good.

Many of the people passing Chino greeted him or stopped to ask about some community problem or report on some ongoing activity. It appeared he was very much a public figure. Mentioning this to him caused his large frame and broad face to dissolve into a thoughtful expression. He settled on the stoop steps and looked down the street and then back. "Yeah, people used to know me for really fucked up things. Now, I dig them knowing me for trying to get it together." Again, that satisfying laugh rumbled out of him as he waved to a couple across the street. They eagerly waved and smiled back.

Seeing Chino sitting on his tenement building's front stoop, it would be difficult to imagine this twenty-six-year-old young man had been one of the most feared gang-leaders the Lower East Side had ever known. He now looks so benign and passive in his panda-bear-ish portliness. His thick nappy black beard and modified Afro hair style in sharp contrast to the sick and sleek young "war lord" appearance of his teen years.

Early photos show his under six-foot frame standing erect and proud. None of the pride has left him but sizable bulk has now covered his tallish figure. His small dark eyes still have the alertness that years of "protecting" his turf necessitated. Chino's gaze today is one of inspection rather than a greeting.

Chino drained the rest of his beer. He rose from the stoop and walked across the street to the neighborhood bodega-grocery store. An animated Spanish conversation ensued between Chino and the young owner. A unique sense of warmth passed between these two young men. A feeling of belonging and shared experience was evident.

With a fresh can of beer and a ham and cheese sandwich, Chino crossed back to his stoop. He looked as comfortable sitting on the stoop as another would be sitting in his living room. But his years of experience as a "street-person" had made this Chino's living room.

The youngest of five children (three brothers and one sister) of parents who worked five or six days a week, Chino basically was on his own from early childhood. He had learned street ways during a childhood in the Chelsea section of New York's West Side. For protection and camaraderie, he had joined a neighborhood gang, the Assassins, when he was almost eleven. Chino's keen judgment, awareness, and political shrewdness had quickly elevated him to a position of warlord. It was his responsibility to keep peace with rival gangs or to negotiate the terms of "battle." And many a battle there had been. He became adept at quickly judging people and situations. This ability would be used adroitly in the community action work initiated in the Real Great Society and CHARAS.

A teenaged young man calls out to Chino. He crosses over to the stoop and sits. They grasp each other's hand in the "brother" handshake. "What's happening, brother?" Chino intones. A short whispered conversation ensues. The young man's older brother has been picked up on a narcotics charge. He's being held in jail for the use and possession of heroin. But this time, the older brother wants to really "kick." Chino agrees it's a good idea and states he'll try to get to the right people and place the addict into a drug rehabilitation program.

Chino places his arm around the distraught young man's shoulders. Chino's voice is soft and comforting. "Man, some of my brothers went into drugs and the whole narcotic problem for many years of their lives. They made my mother suffer a lot. But now they are okay. Some are going to college. They all have dependable jobs. Now my father feels he has accomplished his responsibility. He gonna be retiring soon from years of being a waiter and my mother is gonna stop working in the bra factory. They are going back to P.R. and my father feels confident that he doesn't have to worry about us anymore."

The young man nodded his understanding and thanked Chino for his forthcoming efforts. Chino laughed as he continued, "The person that worries my father most now is me. Because I'm always into some creative thing. He wants me to have something steady." The young man laughed along with Chino and grasped Chino's hand in the "brother" handshake and again, thanked him and walked away.

Chino watched the young man disappear down the street. He shook his head reflectively. "You know, it's good to see guys like that really interested in trying to help someone in his family. Too many people today are only for number one, themselves and no one else. A lot of people knock the family today. I've thought about this and believe that the more industrial certain nations have become, the less importance was given the family structure. I'm not against industrial development, but I'm in favor of the family. That's what the gangs were really into. Substitute families. With nearly everyone's family out working or the apartment so loaded with kids, a lot of people escaped to the streets to find new families geared to what they needed.

"The family with a sense of common care has to be revived in an urban society. An urban society has to develop a new concept of strong family contact. We had that contact in the street gangs. I mean we took care of each other. That's the beginning. Even when brothers belonged to different gangs and would fight each other, when they got home they used to love each other, no matter how crazy it sounds.

"Street gangs, for me, was part of my university education. My ability at leadership and things like that was learned in the gangs. My ability to understand other people began there. I began analyzing things there. The gang was really, in a funny way, the beginning of community involvement. A lot of people see the gangs negatively; some see it from a positive viewpoint. To me it was a positive involvement. I do not regret the things I did then. I would hate to do them now, because my mind is different. But I cannot regret my past. Regretting my past is like giving up on my life. My past is my past."

Having finished his sandwich and beer, Chino now arose and walked down towards Avenue A through the many people moving up and down the block. "Man, these streets are a whole life experience. I'm now using techniques I learned when I was a gang leader. You know, it's a simple decision to make. You destroy things or you build them. And you got to make that decision. My decision is now to build things. There are a lot of brothers and sisters down here who would like to stay in a destruction bag. That's where they are. But if they don't want no help, there's nothing you can do about it. The way I see things is that I'm available for whoever wants to change. But I'm not gonna force nobody to change. In my own life now, if I want to change, I go someplace to learn what I need or just try to change."

Walking uptown on Avenue A, a notch of obvious junkies was nestled together in front of a run-down luncheonette. They ranged in age from middle teens to late forties. One or two looked up and called out, "What's happening, brother," and dropped back into their mindless staring. Chino's eyes revealed despair and sadness. These were his brothers, regardless of their current state. "Funny thing about the early days of the gangs," Chino began. "There wasn't any real junk around in those days. But, later, when some of the leaders became junkies, like the idols of the members, then a lot of the brothers followed along. Man, 90 percent of the gangs became junkies." His voice was now tinged with bitterness. "The thing that really knocked off the gangs was dope."

Approaching the Peoples Park at 7th Street and Avenue A, many young boys and girls who had emptied out of the nearby school were busy running about and enjoying themselves in an area that the community had established through its own energies. Again, many of the kids in the park and several adults came over to speak to Chino. There was much amiable conversation in Spanish and English. A general feeling of "good vibes" was generated back and forth. Despite all the litter in the streets and the general decay of the area, the feeling among people seemed positive. It was clear evidence that depressed conditions did not dim sparks of hope for alternatives. The Peoples Park was a testimonial to such efforts.

"Ain't this something." Chino enjoyed walking through this space. It was a product of everything he was attempting to represent for nearly the last ten years. He sat down on the steps of the small stage that edged the northern line of the Park. He waved his hand, trying to encompass the whole area. "Man, I don't think something like this could have happened if the gangs, that is those who didn't get into junk or any other shit, hadn't changed their directions. The gang structure in the early 60s had to go somewhere because the social atmosphere of this area was changing. There was like two big alternatives: drugs or putting all your energies into some creativity, some positive direction.

"I went with this direction because I like to see things be creative and things to be built, not ripped up. I sometimes think that being run out of New York back when I was seventeen was the best fuckin' thing that ever happened to me." Chino's expression was grave. He was twisting his beard into little knots of hair with his right hand. Remembering the particulars of that situation brought a tension to Chino's voice. His usual lilting accented voice was now flat and exact.

"You know, I sort of got pressure to leave for P.R. And I did. It was best I do that because a lot of our people was getting away with murder. A lot of crimes were being committed. And, you know, it's hard to convict us." He now began to chuckle heartily. "And when I used to get arrested it was for something I didn't do. But I don't want to complain because I committed so many things when I was young. I got to the point where I didn't object when I was pulled in because there was so much I had gotten away with. But there are a lot of brothers in prison that haven't committed any crime. But those cops just pick you up for fuckin' things you don' do.

"But my case it worked out different. The cops at the precinct told me, 'Leave.' And it took me one hour to pack up and split. I know what they can do to you. I seen times when they put dope in people's pockets. Look, there's a lot of police that are very good fuckin' people and there are lot of bastards.

"I was glad to be able to return to P.R. I had a more positive view of everything I was doing there. It was exciting and beautiful. I had all kinds of jobs and travelled through the whole island. I was free, nobody bothered me. I wasn't responsible to nobody. I had a great fuckin' time there. Actual freedom. I felt great about it. I also began viewing the local political activities and learning from them. Just looking at them and learning. I must have spent nearly a year and a half there. But then I came back and started fuckin' around again, in the streets. I found most of my gang brothers were junkies. I had to decide to go this way or that way."

Chino was now very tense. His knotting of his beard became more agitated as his fingers twisted through the black, nappy hairs. He suddenly turned and said, "And man, I found out that a few of my own brothers had turned to junk. Right in my own family. It cut deep. And I had two choices: dope or try to be as creative as possible. Listen, a lot of brothers tried and fell into the alligator pit. Me and the guys coming with me, well, we fell into the mushroom pit."

Chino now realized it was past 3 P.M. and he should be checking into the NENA offices on Avenue C between 3rd and 4th Streets. He got up and started a healthy pace towards the storefront converted office space. NENA is a community action group that involves itself with the housing, health, recreation, day-care and myriad other problems besetting the people living in a blighted ghetto area. Chino works as general trouble shooter and consultant.

The office is divided into various partitioned work areas. Chino enters and greets everyone he encounters with "What's happenin' brother?" The young woman at the reception desk is busy on the phone talking to someone in Spanish. She hands Chino a number of messages as he passes her desk. He scans them and says, 'Thanks, sister" to the still busy young woman and turns into his little cubicle. He quickly gets on the phone. There are calls to be made to one or two city agencies, several local residents, a foundation executive, one of the CHARAS brothers, his wife and his brother Jocko.

Having finished his barrage of phone calls, Chino sits back from the desk and loudly announces for all to hear that he needs a beer and some food. From another cubicle, Robert Nazario, who is a former RGS member, calls back, "Do your thing, brother." There is some playful bantering and intra-cubicle visiting. Chino gathers a small group and all head for a nearby Cuban-Spanish restaurant. The various waiters and counter people seem to know Chino well and greet him with friendly handshakes, talk (in Spanish), and small flourishes of service extended towards the late luncheon group. Chino informs everyone that the waiter will bring out what he thinks is the best food available that day. They'll settle the check later.

The food is sufficient and plentiful, with many rounds of beer for all. Roberto, nicknamed Rabbit, and Chino had begun reminiscing about some of the early days of the gangs and the formation of the RGS group. Chino had mentioned that after his return from Puerto Rico, he had encountered Angelo Gonzalez, "his ace man," at a street party one evening in late autumn of 63 at East 12th Street and Avenue B. Angelo had just come out of prison after three and a half years for a murder rap. Angelo was dissatisfied with his current way of life and Chino had begun to realize his need for a change of direction. It was their encounter and initial talks that formed the basis for the development of the Real Great Society and, later, CHARAS.

Chino was now finishing his fourth beer. He patted his stomach contentedly and allowed a magnificent beer belch to escape to the applause and entertainment of everyone at the table. Chino turned to Rabbit and continued, "You know that Angelo likes to work. Really has to work now to support his batch of kiddies. But, man, he's a hard-working cat working someplace all the time and making money. I'm the godfather to his first daughter. Shame he's not more active with us now." Rabbit smiled a knowing smile, "It's okay. He's taking care of business." Everyone agreed that to be working and providing for your family was better than many of the things they had done in the past or could be doing now as a substitute.

The check arrived and was divided equally among the diners. During the short walk back to the NENA office, Chino began talking about Dr. Charles Slack, who had first worked with the early RGS people. He had then been a Harvard professor of psychology who had devised a study of street gangs operating on the lower West Side of the city. Chino had met and befriended him during those days. When RGS was forming, Chino called upon him for advice and assistance. Charlie (there are no titles or societal appellations in the street gangs), soon became their publicity director and tour arranger (a device used to raise necessary money and attract attention).

"He was a great fuckin' cat, and he probably doesn't know it," Chino was saying expansively. "He's one of the best publicity men around this country. I know that because I seen him in action and the guy is great. He knew how to say the right thing at the right time. Call the right person at the right time. The man was too much. He said he would stay around as long as we needed him and then he would leave. After he did what he thought was his commitment, he left. That cat was too much. We loved him, man."

The NENA offices were somewhat quieter. It was nearly 6 P.M. In about an hour or so those people who work at the NENA office would be arriving and the neighborhood people would be flowing in for meetings or discussions about the multifaceted problems facing these ghetto dwellers. Chino sat in his little office quietly for a time, going over some papers, and making some notes. He then just sat, seemingly in deep thought. A phone rang and Chino answered it. He took the message and hung up. "It's just like the early days at RGS. This guy has an idea he wants to discuss with the board. We used to get ideas from everybody. We'd listen to anyone. Listen to a hundred and maybe you'll come up with one good one. We used to have meetings with over two hundred people and it looked like every-one had an idea for us to do. But fuck it, whatever came across was what's important. A thousand people talk and you get ten good ideas from them, that's great.

"One of the main things we kept coming up with was that we needed more than we knew. Education became important. But we wanted each person to educate himself. And, you know, some of these guys are now lawyers and into other heavy professions. I learned by going to different individuals that knew what I wanted to know and I'd ask them. I also took special courses that people sug-gested so I'd improve my basic education. Learned to read and write when I was nearly nineteen but I learned.

"My responsibility was to my self-education and how to learn at my convenience regardless of the system. Many of the brothers who were with us then and have done good come around to help other people in any way they can. These are the guys that are all right. Some other people get into a bag of self-interest and only think of themselves. I think they get lost, sometimes. Only see the now and not what can be around the corner. It's tough to stay in the struggle, I know that. But you have to hang in."

Rabbit poked his head in and said there was a quick meeting being called. Chino was gone about twenty minutes and returned, laughing quietly. The meeting had been called to decide upon some name for a neighborhood project that was being planned by the NENA staff. This meeting had reminded Chino of the time a name was needed for the group he and Angelo had gathered around them. "We had a meeting like this one because we couldn't consider calling ourselves the Assassins or the Dragons. It has to be a name to blow fuckin' people's minds. So a whole bunch of names came about. You know, for a time we was calling ourselves the Spartican Army. But that wasn't much an enthusiastic name because people used to react to it in a funny way. We were having this meeting on the top floor of 605 East 6th Street. Different people started calling out different names. There was also some criticism involving the Johnson Administration and the way they kept hiring all those high-priced cats to work in our community. They really didn't know shit about us. And then some people screamed out 'Down with the great society.' And then someone yelled out, 'Yeah, up with the real great society.' And everything broke up with people shouting 'That's it. We are the Real Great Society.' It was a spontaneous creation. It was the same when the six brothers got together to talk about forming what became CHARAS. We knew a name was important because people symbolize themselves behind a name. And the idea of using our first initials came up. We juggled them around and finally out came C-H-A-R-A-S. It could mean anything. Later we did find out from some kid that Charas, in Indian, means hash. Well, that's way things happen sometime.

"You know there was something else from the meeting I just had that made me think of some of the early problems we had with RGS. This project is a teenage summer program dealing with recycling paper and tin cans. We had to decide if it should be a regular business set-up or some kind of non-profit arrangement. That was our hang-up in the early RGS days. We got into business programs to support our community programs. Our purpose was to try to get to be self-supported. It's like a nation wants to be independent of the United States but it still economically counts on the United States. It's not an independent country.

"And after several years we realized it wasn't a good idea for us to work that way. To become a self-sustaining organization that could service other people in the community would mean we'd have to create some kind of General Motors. And in order to be a good businessman and have a good profitable business, you have to be a bastard. I think in this society the owners have to be bastards. They have to kick the other guy in order to make it.

"And the same is true of politics. We made it very clear we could not get involved in political events. Politics isolates you into one goal instead of being flexible in dealing with the reality of trying to do whatever you want to do. We also knew that we could not get involved in every novel event that happens. If we see the future as a point of development, then any type of political involvement (no matter how radical or how conservative) delays you from actually producing, taking care of business, of being responsible to help out your brothers and sisters. Whatever politics we get into ourselves does not mean the organization was getting involved. We have the same policy at CHARAS and also now at NENA. Look, it's too early yet to run into any brick walls. So we don't want to make no mistake. Brick walls hurt and when they hurt, they hurt. That's why we try to avoid that kind of action."

People began arriving at the storefront offices. The sudden babble of conversations and phones ringing was in sharp contrast to the near quiet of the past hour. Chino was now being called from meting to meeting, or pulled aside by different men or women wanting to talk about their problems or ideas. It was an active and vigorous three hours that followed. By 10 P.M. everyone, NENA workers and the neighborhood people, looked slightly haggard. Chino looked sweaty and tired. He was still expected to work an eight-hour shift for the taxi company, beginning at midnight.

"Wow, man, this was a heavy night. Let's get a beer." Chino was walking out the door when he was stopped again for a hurried fifteen-minute conference with some people. He finally came over to the front door and looked up and down Avenue C. "You know," he said, "it would be nice if CHARAS could get enough money so that I could spend all my time there instead of just jumping back and forth like I do now. Because I would like to get into heavy ventures of new ways of life for communities. The dome was something we wanted to get involved with to do just to know we could do it. If we were able to do that, we could do anything we're determined to do.

"Now, it's like the second part of CHARAS. It's going to begin this year. We want to investigate communal life. This is now our changing period. Actually, we always had it, since the beginning of 64. We have the experience of our actions. That's what we want to do this coming decade. Put this experience into action. We are now at a stage when we have to look at things—economically, politically, and culturally from different ways. We have to see what we can do as a community and deal with it. We have to see the different things people can do as communities.

"So the whole thing is getting our people in this community involved with something different from what they know now. Showing them you don't have to be the same old person over and over again like a broken record. We have to find ways to show them they are people with minds. That they have or could get some great way of doing something. I can see a fantastic community develop from something like that. Sure most of the people would want to get involved. That's okay. They'll see how much better we're living and want to join us.

"Our thing is to teach in this decade. We have to spend a lot of time teaching what we have learned to show somebody else how it was done in the past and how they can do it in their present and future. We can be this tool for others. That's what I see us doing in the 70s."

Chino was headed back to the little bodega from which he had earlier gotten his "breakfast" sandwich. He was going to get some beers and cross the street into his building to spend an hour or two with his wife who would tell him of her activities in another community action group for which she works. They would have this short interval before Chino had to pick up his cab for the evening. The day had been long and filled with activities and events that kept this young man alert and engaged. He wouldn't want it any other way. And Ruth, to be sure, would want no other life for herself and Chino except the continued fulfillment of their dream of a better tomorrow and their efforts towards its hopeful achievement.

Humberto Crespo

Reports about a person from various sources do not usually have a consistency of attitude. We seldom live in a world that has mirrors facing each other with endless reflections of the same image. But this appears to be the quality of Humberto Crespo.

He grew up with Chino and Angelo in the cauldron of the Lower East Side, infested with the gangs and creeping lure of drugs. He used the military as an escape from a life of entrenched hopelessness. In this, he was not unique.

Unlike many of his confreres, Humberto came back to his old haunts and friends, finding both the best and worst possibilities available to him. Many of his friends turned to junk. Others had attempted to help discover ways of combating the evils of the ghetto. He wanted action. He, therefore, wheedled, cajoled, prodded those who offered positive alternatives.

He occasionally faltered when action was not as immediate as he desired. He played with junk like the cat with the end of a thread. But when he was involved and dedicated, Crespo was a dynamic force in the pursuit of programs or ideas that could help his people.

He made a deep impression upon those who knew him. Their lives were touched by his humor and vitality. There was a sense of true potential in this young man whose life ended as he was attempting to help another sufferer.

His friends' recollections of him speak best for him. By sharing their thoughts they close the gap again.

As remembered by CHINO GARCIA:

"Crespo, I think he was a year older than me or a year younger than me. It's not important, the age. He died in August, 1970. I was in New Mexico at that time. Crespo was a very interesting person. The cat was an evangelist. He kind of looked at life as a development process... one of the things I dug about the brother was he looked at life as something new always and you never have to do the same thing over and over again. A lot of us work ourselves like that.

"At one time in his life he was a very Goldwater-type of person. Yeah! Conservative. Crespo always liked to be different than the in-crowd just so he could bug people at the right time. You have to look at yourself when people are like that. Now, the brother joined the Marines because he was proud of being in the service of the United States. At that time there was thousands of young people who wanted to be a Marine because it makes you a great man. I think through the Marines he became a menace. According to what he had explained to me, he had a fantastic military life. He's a legend, according to what his friends told me and what he had told me.

"He and me was involved in the Assassins together. We grew up together. We had a great time as members of the Assassins. We had a great time as teenagers. We went everywhere together and made it with a lot of sisters. We had a great time. When he came out of the Marines, he still was a little bit in favor of the Vietnamese war... but not as before. He served a year in Vietnam in active combat. He saw a lot of fuck-ups there. He joined a couple of the Veterans of the Vietnam Movements because he was very sick and tired of the war. He noticed the game being played on him.

"So the reason he became an active person in CHARAS is, I feel, that he wanted to be part of creating an alternative. One of the most important things about the brother is he was the most... active member of the organization. The reason he was is because he didn't give a hell about too much structure or discipline. So, therefore, he became a flamboyant type of character.

"Yeah! He had a great time, had a beautiful time and enjoyed himself. Everybody liked him. He was a lot of fun. He always used to come out with a lot of jokes. He hardly ever said no to anything. He went to every place he was asked. He also took every drug you could think of. Just to try it. Not as an addict but so he could try it. He was the type of cat that wanted to have the experience before he talks to you about it. The reason he finally went against the war was because he was in the war. The reason he didn't go on buying heroin was because he took heroin and he knew thousands of people involved in that drug. The reason he could talk to people about acid was because he took acid. Before he gave his opinion about something, he tried to know about it from his own experience. If he never tried it, he hardly never gave his opinion.

"Crespo was around 5' 5"." He had dirty blond hair, light green eyes. He was light-skinned Puerto Rican. He had a big head and jaw. He had a good build physically. He never got dressed up but he always had a clean shirt and clean pair of pants on. He kept himself pretty clean, not dressed up but always clean. His father is Puerto Rican, his mother is Cuban. She speaks Spanish and English and writes it very well. Crespo identified very much with his Caribbean and Puerto Rican background and culture. He was a very intelligent person. I mean intelligent.

"And, like every young man, the future college event became an important part of his life. But after awhile he started thinking more of the social structure of our society. I think he would have dedicated his life to changing the social structure into something having more humanized ways of life. In a way, that was how he got killed. There was a brother member, Sanchez. He was addicted. He started kicking cold turkey. He realized, in order to keep away from drugs, he would probably have to go to a different environment. So Crespo said, look, I know some people in Florida and maybe they will help you out. You could stay with them and they will help you out. And, he said, at the same time I go visit my family down there. He told the guy, let's hitch-hike there. So they started hitchhiking. A few days before he left he was telling a few of the fellows that he really didn't feel like going, that something had told him not to go on the trip. It's strange when people get that kind of feeling.

"Yeah! He told his closest friends besides me. I wasn't around because of a trip to Mexico so eventually he went with brother Sanchez. On their way to Florida, there was a terrible car accident involving a few other cars and he met his death there.

"The most important influence that he had on the development of CHARAS was that he had a question for everything that was said. I never heard any mother-fucker ask as many questions like he did. He was that type of character. Why, why this, why that. I think that was his big influence. Because you know that when you're going to be with that person, you really gotta have a lot of fuckin answers. He asked you more why's than you probably ever heard in your life. I think that was important."

As remembered by ANGELO GONZALES JR:

"Well, Crespo and me went back to the gang days. He was there in the projects also. His family still lives here. He used to run with Chino a lot during the days of the Assassins. Crespo had a hitch in the Marines after he started to fool around with drugs. He got too serious into it. Anyway, enough so he couldn't get out of it. At that time the Marines was the best place for him. It was and it wasn't. It got him out of the dope. But he got into a lot of trouble with the Marine Corps because he was really a rebel to that whole system, basically. He was always asking why. Like Chino says, you don't ask why in the Marine Corps. Especially not to your first master sergeant of the drill. You just keep your mouth shut. He never kept his mouth shut. But he went through the whole trip with the Marine Corps. He did a lot of traveling and served a lot of time in the brig. He did a lot of crazy things and then he came out.

"He had a big 'why' all about him. He kept asking questions. The Marine Corps is not working, this is not working, what will work, what should I do. He had the GI benefits so he had better go to school. He tried that out for a while also. He liked it and he didn't like it.

"I can't remember if he went to N.Y.U. or Manhattan Community. I don't know. I'm not sure because he was more out of school than in school. We were trying to get Crespo to get down with us because most of the time he just wasn't doing anything and he had a lot of energy and we felt that he could... once... he's the type of guy that once he wants to do something, he could really get it done. So finally when we talked about Mexico and the Outward Bound trip he got excited. He was very bad in the in-between stages. He was very impatient. He'd come around and talk but want action fast.

"I talked to him about Outward Bound and he said he had experience in the Marine Corps. He compared that with Outward Bound. I told him it was completely different. In the Marine Corps you had to do whatever you were ordered. At Outward Bound it was completely different. You don't have to do it if you don't want to. But once we got into things (that's me, Crespo, and Moses) in Colorado and Mexico it was okay. Then one particular thing came up that was kind of interesting. The Indians we were supposed to innoculate never knew that we was supposed to innoculate them. So when we showed up, they were really frightened. They were raised detached from any real civilization. They were really in the mountains. We were already imposing on them, it turned out to be. Crespo really got uptight about that. So did the rest of us. Crespo really made an effort to communicate with them, make them feel at ease or else leave if we couldn't do that. If we couldn't try to make ourselves acceptable to them then we shouldn't be there. That came off pretty good. Like Crespo was really a humanistic guy. Like, he could really get into people's souls. Any place he went, he was like a real force. He managed, somehow, to really be able to give, to relate to it or do something for it. If he dug something, he really got into it all the way.

"I don't know what else to say about the guy except that we all loved him a lot. We did a lot of crazy things together. But at the end of his life he was into doing new and different things, trying to know if they could happen if he put enough energy into it. He was so dissatisfied with what exited that he just couldn't accept it. No way, from the Marine Corps on down."

As remembered by ROY BATTISTE:

"I met Crespo probably around November, 1969 when he had just gotten out of the service and he came in to work at CHARAS. I'd known him before then but we didn't talk or anything like that. It was just on a hello-goodbye kind of basis. He was good friends with Chino and Angelo and he didn't have anything to do when he got out of the service. So this was something to do.

"You know, he didn't take any shit, kind of kept Chino and Angelo on their toes all the time by questioning them. He was not afraid to tell them go 'fuck off' if they were sitting around. He'd been in Vietnam and seen a lot of guff and came back to the States. He was away for a few years and things had changed dramatically. At that time, a lot of his friends were messing around with dope and it was frustrating to him to see a lot of this.

"He came back and he'd work for us for awhile and he began experiencing frustrations within himself and started hanging out with a lot of his old friends who were messing around with dope. Hang around with people messing with dope and you're going to start using dope too. That may have led to his eventual death. But before that he was pretty active. Working pretty hard in the beginning trying to get himself together. Then he went down to Colorado and Mexico with us.

"It was a good experience for him. He came back with a lot of positive attitudes but began to feel frustrated again. He didn't have any money at that time and it became a question of how he was going to survive. He had a good relationship with his family but they didn't have the answers to the questions that he had. Nobody had an answer for him. We used to talk about it.

"He was looking for himself. You have to understand it's a heavy shock when you get out of the service and are working to try and pick up the pieces. It's like when you move out of your neighborhood, you leave behind your whole life. Experiences become different. In order to survive, you have to make a lot of changes in yourself, especially from the military to civilian life. It's kind of hard to get back into the normal grind as you knew it. He often seemed happy and outgoing but that's what he did to fight off the blues. I knew him in other moments when he was completely down and out.

"But, above all, he was a really compassionate person. He really cared about people. He tried to help someone else. When we were in Mexico, the way he related to people there. He really dug what he was doing. He dug the people he got involved with. Yet within himself there was a lot of turmoil going on. But he wanted to see things work out positively and he tried to do everything he could to make that kind of positive change."

As remembered by MOSES ANTHONY FIGUEROA:

"One day Chino came over to the house and said Moses, this is Crespo. He just came back from Vietnam. This was in 69, the end of 69, and he said, you know Crespo is going to be part of us. Crespo said, now dig it you guys, you guys have been doing all those things together. And what I am going to do is going to hang out with you guys and learn because I was in Vietnam and while I was there my mind opened up to a lot of things and I have a lot of skills to offer. But as far as civilian life is concerned, I knew very little. I am here to learn. I looked into Crespo's eyes, there was a very strong spark of fire in his eyes.

"His eyes were sort of green. A very rich sort of green-gray with yellow dots that whenever he got excited, the yellow in the eyes would play in the light. He had short hair, long in the back. He came to my house wearing Army clothes and Army boots, which as far as I knew he always wore. Then one day we were just together. I said come up to my house and we'll eat. He came and he stayed all day. He came around 11 A.M. and he left around 7 P.M. We talked about what had been happening, those days in Vietnam. War was the big thing. He had just come back from it.

"Then we talked and he remembered a lot about Puerto Rico and Puerto Rican life. I think that's where the strength of our relation-ship lay: the fact that we were both men that had been carved out of Puerto Rico rather than men who had been carved into a Puerto Rican culture in New York City. We both lived in two different kinds of culture, Puerto Rican culture in New York and Puerto Rican culture in Puerto Rico. Those are different levels of communication that not many Puerto Ricans have. Chino has it, Angelo has it, Rabbit has it, Little Rabbit has it. He had that and I think that's where our strong binding force comes in. Crespo surely had that and with his experi-ence in Vietnam, Crespo was a whole different kind of man.

"I just felt good being around Crespo. Crespo was very shy in many ways. I don't know if he showed this to other people or not but one day when I lived on 88th Street, right off the park, he came in with this beautiful creature, this Puerto Rican girl. She was just an amazing little creature. I had never seen a Puerto Rican woman in New York like that. She wasn't a big woman. She was around 5' 4" and her features were very strong. But they were features of a Puerto Rican woman from Puerto Rico, like the kind of women I know. He said this is my girlfriend and then he introduced her. We spent the afternoon together. Crespo was always alive. That's what I liked about Crespo. Many people criticize people who are always on but Crespo in the beginning was very gentle and he never made me feel uptight. I never felt in any way ego-conflicted with Crespo. And Crespo was a man and a half. He'd been in Vietnam, he shot people, he'd been shot at, but yet there was this unique simplicity that came out of him in childlike quality.

"I don't know if Crespo understood the concept of the geodesic dome and all the technology that was beginning to flow through the group. But he would say, I don't know what the fuck you guys are talking about. Let's just do it. What do you want me to do? That's the way he was and that's why I liked him so much."

As remembered by SAL BECKER:

"Crespo and I met at CHARAS when we went on the Outward Bound trip. I wasn't one of the guys that grew up with him, like Angelo and Chino. Angelo and I had spent about four days driving. I don't drive. So he was doing all the driving and we were exhausted and tired and like run down. Like, we just wanted to get to Colorado, get our equipment, and get someone else to drive us or send us to Mexico. When we got to Denver, we found that we would have to do another half hour or 45 minutes to get to Colorado Springs where the group was. Crespo was already there. When we got to Colorado Springs, we parked the car at the bottom of the mountain and one of the assistant instructors drove us up to the top. The first thing that happened, when we got out of the truck, was seeing all these strange people from Outward Bound looking at us and checking us out, wondering why we were late. Like it's taboo to be late for an Outward Bound course. Well, we see all these strange people looking at us and from out of the blue, Crespo comes running. He grabs me and hugs me and says, Sal baby, what's happening. Like, I never knew him that well but I got such a warm reception from him. Right then and there our true full relationship started because I said, wow, man, this guy is really beautiful.

"I never had the opportunity to get to know him that well because we were working ten blocks from each other in New York. He showed me that he had been through a lot of changes and he learned from his changes. He didn't want everybody else to go through the same shit that he went through. So, if he would see you uptight, he would try to rap to you. He was available to talk to if you needed someone to lean on. But everyone at CHARAS tried to be like that.

"When I stop to think now, Crespo never had a negative attitude. He was always such a happy-go-lucky guy. He'd get pissed off sometimes when something went wrong, he'd say, fuck it, let's do it again.

"I didn't know he was once totally involved in drugs until after he died. I can understand that if he did. It was because his degree came from the university of the streets, I mean the real streets. He had learned to deal with people, all people. And when I was with him I didn't know I was white. It was fantastic.

129

Angelo Gonzalez, Jr.

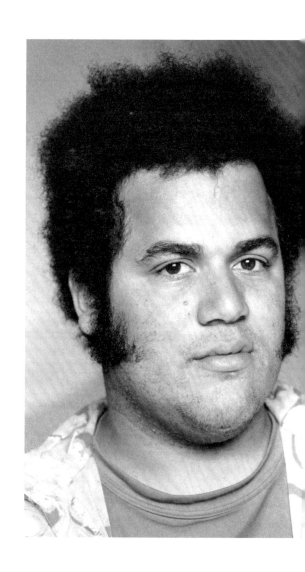

Angelo, twenty-eight now, seems to be a tranquil, mild-mannered young man—a surprising observation given his early background. None of the turbulent, violent, anti-social, and highly aggressive behavior appears to be operative today. If social and psychological reformation is possible, Angelo is an excellent example of the process.

In his teens, Angelo Gonzalez, Jr. was a lean, hard-bodied young man with a taut, handsome Latin face and limpid, brown, saucer-like eyes. Although not tall, he stood like a giant among his peers on the Lower East Side in the late 50s. Angelo was the undisputed gang leader of over 800 young men and women who comprised the two gangs known as the Assassins and the Dragons. What is more remarkable is that Angelo acquired this power when he was thirteen years old.

Today, with the years of gang fighting behind him, a murder rap at the age of 15, and over three years in prison, the co-organizer of the Real Great Society and CHARAS has put on some weight and his strong-featured face has softened. Although his energy may have lessened somewhat over the years, his desire for new societal patterns is still passionate.

At present, Angelo has no permanent residence. When in New York City, he usually shuttles from his mother's home in the Baruch Projects of the Lower East Side to one of the several women who consider him their "man." In the past, he had been thought of as a "prize catch." His reputation is still very strong and there are many available women with whom Angelo takes up temporary residence. There are also a number of children in addition to the two daughters from his first marriage. Angelo feels responsible to all of these offspring. There has been, therefore, a constant need to bolster his personal finances to support his various familial responsibilities. Most recently, Angelo worked as an oil truck delivery man during the winter months. He was on an unending schedule of overtime work to raise his take-home salary. The resulting complexity of his private life for the past three or four years has curtailed his full association with the ongoing activities of the Real Great Society and CHARAS.

He is now involved with a group of young men who own a 350-acre farm in upper New York State. They are eagerly seeking to formulate procedures to make this property more socially productive for people from areas like the Lower East Side or any other low-income ghetto area. Angelo is acting as an adviser and participant in whatever plans evolve. He is now spending considerable time reconstructing the main house and subsidiary units on the property. The owners of the farm are working with Angelo in this basic work while they discuss the future of the venture. Angelo also recruits friends from the Lower East Side to help in construction work. It gives them a chance to live in the country for a while and to "cool out" their heads from all the city hassles.

It was during one of Angelo's infrequent trips home that he sat and rapped about his past, present and future. He was at the housing project apartment of the most recent young woman, Evelyn, with whom he was spending time. Their two-month old son was lying peaceably on the worn couch attended to by Evelyn's mother. It was early on a gray May morning. Angelo, fighting a severe head cold, was tired. He had his coffee in the overcrowded kitchen filled with extra chairs and baby clothes drying over the open gas range. A McDonald's apple turnover was mistakenly put into the oven in its cardboard package and was in the process of burning. Money was needed for baby food and cigarettes. Angelo complained about this, but handed Evelyn the money for these immediate necessities. The TV was blasting in the living room. A gentle older man was seated in front of the set but was not really watching. He was never introduced. While Angelo was having his coffee, a young man with sleep-filled eyes weaved into the kitchen. It was Evelyn's younger brother. He said nothing to anyone. He merely heated some water in a discarded large tin can and sat at the table impassively waiting.

Angelo explained that he wanted to get back to the farm as quickly as possible. He'd borrowed one of the guy's pick-up trucks to get into the city. Angelo knew it was needed back on the farm for the many chores that were being done. His own car had been damaged in an accident the previous week. Fortunately, no one was seriously hurt. The only occupant of the car needing any medical attention was Chino Garcia's older brother, Paco. Angelo was unhurt but angry at the expense of having to repair the car. He wasn't sure how he would get the money. It was only one more pressing problem with which Angelo would have to deal.

Angelo explained that his heavy schedule of constant work during the winter had made contact difficult. He was also somewhat hesitant talking about his past to anyone again. Angelo felt that, too often, his words, thoughts, or intentions had been confused or sensationalized. He readily conceded that his past had been wild and unusual, but he felt that his unusual behavior did not fully reflect his personality, neither in his youth nor, particularly, now. He finally concluded he would cooperate if what he said was used directly as related.

By this time, Evelyn had returned from her quick shopping errand. She hurriedly began to prepare the infant's food. Angelo suggested the conversation be held in one of the three bedrooms, away from the noise and confusion of the household. The bedroom was extremely cold. A broken window had not been repaired and the unusually harsh May winds savagely whistled through it. Angelo called out for some tea and settled back on one of the two blue cotton, chenille-covered beds and indicated that he was now ready. His voice, usually gravelly, was now even more rasping in tone. The cold had made his eyes watery. There was a weariness in his body. When he lay back on the bed, he seemed to be drifting off to sleep. He caught himself very quickly and sat up abruptly. He pulled a sweater over his graying T-shirt to ward off the cold. The door opened and Evelyn brought in the tea and asked about some domestic problem. Angelo's eyes grew angry. He told her not to bother him again until he was finished.

He settled back onto the bed while sipping his tea. He looked up and said, smiling, "O.K. Let's get that fucking thing going."

Angelo, where and when were you born?

I was born in New York in October, 1945. My family lived in East Harlem at the time. Spanish Harlem. I actually was born on Welfare Island.

You began school in East Harlem?

No! We used to move around quite a bit, like we lived in East Harlem, in Coney Island, Rockaway. When I was five years old I started school in Coney Island.

How old were you when you moved to the Lower East Side?

About thirteen. And I went to school over here, public school, for about a few months and then I went to Catholic school, and then I finished Catholic school and went to one year of high school, not even one year... never finished that first year.

What high school was that?

Wilke Auto, for automotive mechanics on Bedford Avenue in Brooklyn. But mostly during that time I was in school, there was a lot of gangs around. And then I got busted. That's why I didn't finish high school. I probably wouldn't have finished anyway because I didn't dig it. I went from high school to jail and then from jail to the beginning of the organizations.

What was the bust for?

Homicide, murder. I don't want to talk about it any further. That's what it was about... it was an armed robbery in these projects, and we killed a guy.

How old were you?

Fifteen–and some boy is still doing time on that. He and this other dude got busted and he got life and I got off because I was under-age and stuff like that. I did time, but not as much time as if I was sixteen years old. Then when I got out of jail, me and Chino hooked up.

When you moved into this neighborhood at thirteen, you moved into an already established gang structure. How did you relate to that situation?

The reason I was prompted to start a gang as opposed to getting into one was I don't particularly dig taking orders from people and stuff like that. I didn't dig that scene. I almost got shot by a group of guys, the Sportsmen, who thought I was in the Dragons because one of the leaders lived in my building.

Were the Sportsmen basically a black gang?

Yeah! The Dragons was Puerto Rican although one of the leaders of the Dragons was a black dude and they wanted him especially because he should have been with the black guys but he was with us. They thought I was one of his bodyguards. They stopped me and then shot at me with a gun that didn't go off. Then, when I started running, the gun did go off. I didn't want that to happen no more so me and a few people started our own group.

What was the average age of these people?

Anywhere from sometimes eleven years old to like thirteen years old.

You were thirteen when you began your own gang?

Right!

And that was called...

The Dragons. It was one of the divisions of the Dragons. The older guys, who were like the really old Dragons, had built a strong predominantly Puerto Rican group. The Sportsmen were a big black group. But we was split up in divisions. So were the Sportsmen. Like the real old guys were in the first division and when new guys came in, they went into different divisions. But then we finally broke off and became an independent group.

And what were the ages basically of the group you led?

Anywhere like from eleven, twelve years old to guys about twenty, around there.

So actually at the age of thirteen, you were telling guys that were twenty what to do?

Yeah! A lot of different age groups.

How did you manage, at thirteen, to control those in your gang who were much older than you?

I had just started the group. Guys just joined up because... we lived in these projects. We just took these projects as our territory. Those who lived in this territory, as opposed to belonging to another group which we might someday fight, started to join the group as part of their home. So that involved guys of all ages, girls of all ages. Even though I was younger, things just got done. Mainly the guys of twenty, the older guys, wouldn't so much socialize with us as they would fight with us. When we needed to really start a strong force, a lot of the older guys would be there. Not so much for protectiveness but to be part of a gang when there was some really heavy gang fighting going on. Otherwise he would be drafted into another group or just get fucked up.

So there were really two activities of the gang—one was of a strong social character and the other became a protective system?

Right! Right! Which everybody, because of survival I guess, would get involved in as opposed to just a social type thing. That's how things kinda worked out.

What was the need for a gang?

I think it was very human and very basic. First, people wanted to be together in a place where they could really relate and be able to have somebody to talk to. And to be able to have somebody to do stuff together in our own way of doing stuff. I think that's basically what gangs are all about. (Coughing) It's kinda fucking chilly in this room. It was the human aspect that brought people together. Well, geography-wise, people are together anyway. Like, people have to get together one way or another. You have to hook into something. It kinda comes natural when you're in a situation like this.

Could you explain what you mean by situation?

Where thousands of people are together. Kind of walking over each other and you really don't have a chance to express yourself as you would like to, creatively or otherwise. You're cramped up, like you're really in a very fucked-up situation and you react to it. You have the man on your head, you have your school, you know, and you have your parents on your head. Everybody is doing something to you that you don't want them to do. Out of that comes a rebel attitude in the individual. You react to it as such. That's what happened to us, I guess. Out of those feelings of rebellion we developed a sense of the brotherhood. If somebody needed something, everybody helped get that thing. The protective part of it was people protecting each other, basically, I guess against the outside world and one tends to create his own world so as to live more comfortably. That's basically what it's all about.

What was the area like in the 50s and early 60s?

At that time the majority of the groups were from tenements. The majority of people lived in tenements. This was like the second or third projects that was up at the time. But the tenements, like the way they were so fucked-up, really contributed to our people getting together.

It was better to be on the street than to be inside some of the apartments?

Right! Also there was more happening on the street at all times. You have a lot of energy at that age and you just want to get into everything.

How many people were involved in your Dragons gang while you were the leader?

Oh, it started off with a good twenty people and wound up with about three or four divisions of Dragons which contained about two hundred people each, or something like that.

Did you all ever get together at one time?

Oh, yeah! One time we had a big fight in Central Park and we had like, a lot of people, trainloads of people… Mayor Wagner was speaking that day, police chiefs and stuff like that. A brother group got into trouble and we wanted to help them out. We had baseball bats, we claimed we were playing baseball; but it was a sawed-off shotgun right in the middle of all that and the cops were looking all around and couldn't find it. It was a whole scene there. We were commandeering the rowboats from people in Central Park Lake. You know, like sticking them up with shotguns and bow and arrows and all kinds of shit. And taking the boats away from them. Some people actually jumped out of their boats and swam ashore leaving their boats to float there. We could come out and get those boats and fool around.

When did this happen?

In 60, in May. Yeah! In Central Park. You would see the mayor talking or somebody official like that at the Band Shell. There was a whole bunch of people and all of a sudden, guys chasing other guys and all kinds of shit. People running through there and it was wild, man. It was really a fucking scene. Really. We must have had near a thousand people in the park.

Unbelievable. Were there any people killed during that incident?

No. I don't know how that didn't happen. One guy got shot in his ass. Another guy got really messed up. It was a really beautiful day out and I guess nobody really wanted to kill each other, just like, fight with each other. Nobody got killed off.

What was the composition of the opposing gangs?

It was a mixture of everything, because some of our brother groups were included. We finally managed to become brother groups with the blacks. That was the first big thing that happened. Even when I was in jail, that finally turned around and we got together. We broke down a lot of the racism that was involved. It combined as a whole community thing. The majority of the major strong gangs in this particular area of the Lower East Side finally got to be friends. We would be like a big force anytime we had to fight anybody else.

Did you find this was out of necessity or out of a desire to really get together?

Both, actually. The stronger you are the better you could fight. Also, they had a lot of nice girls, and we had a lot of nice girls and, you know, that prompted us to get together.

You wanted their crop...

Right, right, you know, the whole social scene. It was a really nice thing. So basically, that was what was happening with some of the gangs. Some gangs didn't have a lot of people. But they were pretty good because they had really good organization. They had a lot of guns and stuff like that and they were really respected because they knew how to handle themselves pretty well and they didn't want to join other groups.

When you got busted, where were you sent?

First, I was sent to the Men's House of Detention in Manhattan. Then, to the Brooklyn House of Detention, and then when the grand jury dismissed my case... well, actually what they did was transfer my case. Then, I was in the Youth House. From there, I went to Elmira State Prison and from Elmira I went to Coxsackie Prison. That's where I did all my time. It's a minimum security prison in the Catskills.

How much time did you do altogether?

Three and a half years.

So when you got out of prison you were about eighteen?

Right. When I got out that's when I hooked up with Chino again. We got together and started doing things.

What happened significantly during those three and half years?

Personally, I feel that's the greatest education I ever had. I think that's where I got my degree, so-called. I think that's the most real degree there ever is. Frankly, when I went to prison my reputation got there before me. This made things a bit easier because at that time, as opposed to now where all there is in prison are drug addicts, there was nothing but gangbusters, jitterbugs, fighters and stuff like that. Therefore, the structures in prison were set up in gangs, just a continuation. In prison there was gangs. Like, people hear in the House of Detention that other guys get sent up. Like, your friends and your enemies hear about you. That you're coming up. If you have more friends than enemies, it's good. Fortunately for myself, I had more friends than enemies.

And you were considered a heavy?

Yeah! And that kinda helped things out a lot 'cause after the first year I was the main man in charge. I became the president of the Puerto Rican section of the prison. I had a lot of flexibility. Not only with the inmates but also with the administration because they recognize you. They have to. Anytime a potential riot would come up, like you would be the first one they would haul in. Or if they wanted to get at your people, you would be the first one they get in. The point is the place where I did most of my time was really segregated, like an ultra-down-South type of fucked up situation.

You mean the white, the black, the Puerto Ricans were separated from each other.

Right! But the truth was the Puerto Ricans had a little bit more flexibility because of the fact that we could kinda get along with everybody. You know, there are white Puerto Ricans and there are black Puerto Ricans. To a certain degree we had an advantage if we wanted to use it, which we did. It made our time a little easier because we could talk with more people. But one year when I was up there I was one of the youngest guys there. Mostly older guys were there. When I got there actually, I was the youngest guy in the prison. It fell on my birthday also. When I got to Coxsackie, it was my birthday. Anyway, it took me a year to learn the strings, to get into the position as the main man for my people. That made me the spokesman for a large majority of the population. They had told us in the two-week orientation period that the Puerto Rican group had a lot of respect for the administration. We were the minority, but we were also the most respected in the prison. This demanded of us a certain way to act. I was put in a position where I was literally responsible for a lot of people's lives. No one questions the president, no matter what. Not even top lieutenants questioned me. I had just, literally, complete control.

I was also a bit more fortunate because I was transferred to an outside squad, a 12-man dairy squad who worked on the farm. The officer in charge was a guy from Spain. He had heavy Old World type ideas about people... he had a lot of pride in the Latin people. Because we were really the minority there, he wanted to make sure that we carried ourselves as real men. He was the officer in charge a squad of guys who were all Puerto Rican. He would really let us do anything we wanted to do. Like, if you fight inside the institution, you would go into solitude. But outside, he would let us do stuff we could get away with as long as it wasn't inside the institution. Like, if I had to get somebody, or do something, I had a whole lot more flexibility out there since I was a foreman of a squad. So he really like, let me do a lot of stuff. Especially, he really made me able to think about the rest of the group, the decisions I had to make, the people I had to speak to and stuff like that. Really, I had a lot of flexibility. I had some good people with me at that time, like my top lieutenants and stuff. They were really good. They were really able to communicate with people. Physically they were able to handle themselves pretty well, which meant a lot, since most of the Puerto Ricans were kinda small. We managed to survive.

What did you mean when you said that time in this particular prison was like getting a degree?

Well, I was literally put into a situation where I had to deal with the racism in the place and with the administration. I really developed myself into some sort of politician. Being able to carry these three heavy balls, and also maintain my own, that meant really getting heavy with people. It was a really extreme situation in all respects. Like, nobody wanted to deal with each other. But in order to survive, you had to. It was very touchy, very tricky at times. A wrong word or a wrong action would explode into something really nasty. I was under a lot of pressure.

How different was it from the time that you were a gang leader?

You have more flexibility out here in dealing with a situation, space to move around and to do something if necessary. You really have to question the things you do. You have to make some real decisions because when you fuck up in there, you could get killed pretty easy without being able to protect yourself. And the administration can get a hold of you and throw they key away on you.

So the confinement demanded a clearer decision-making pattern.

Right. You have to. Like, you were really up against a lot of things. Out here you are not against those types of things. But, basically, it all turned out pretty good because dealing with the whites and the blacks, my own people and the administration, I began to feel it was about time for people to speak to each other. I thought it was something that was due to happen and somebody had to do it. Somebody had to crack the ice. When I looked at the situation at Coxsackie I realized the position I was in. I felt like I was the best person to begin this rapping.

I did it and it got done to a large degree. Each thing is like an education whether it's intensive or not so intensive. And you really get a chance to look at yourself while you're in prison, as an individual. People never stop to look at themselves to find out what they're really about. If a person can't do that, that person is not working with everything he has. He doesn't know what he has. I was in a position there to do that. To know what I had so I can be better able to deal with the situation I was involved in.

Actually, what you're saying is experience against theory.

Right! And actually accomplishing something through experience. Going through the whole full cycle. I was able to do that and that's why I feel I really earned my degree. Conventionally, when you get a degree, you are able to do a job. I felt I did a job. I know I did a job. I saw… I experienced, through a job, what I could do when I got out. I was geared to do what I did from there on in.

Were there any formal rehabilitation procedures during your stay in jail?

There were a lot of them, but I never did anything with them. Like, they would send me to see some crazy psychiatrist who would ask you what would you do if a battleship was coming down the street. You know, shit like that. So all you did there was set up appointments on your heaviest work days so you could get out of work and speak to him so you don't have to work. Not so much to speak to him but to get out of the job. It was a lot of bullshit.

Was there any type of schooling?

Yeah! We went to half a day of school, half a day of shop because it was a vocational type of prison. It was really a drag, actually. Got into a few things like electrical stuff and the half day of school, book stuff I just didn't get into. Not that I didn't dig reading a lot… I did a lot of reading on my own but like I couldn't do the reading like they wanted you to do. I just couldn't get into it. I was trying to get into people and that whole trip. It was so much more productive and interesting, I feel. That's what I did.

When you were released and came back to the neighborhood, what did you discover?

A lot of dope was around. People was strung out. A lot of people were into a lot of the wrong things and didn't know why. A lot of people were not together and the ones that were together really didn't know what to do.

This was around late 63 and early 64?

Yeah!

The whole drug scene really occurred while you were away?

Around here it did, yeah! When I was an active gang leader I didn't allow none of that shit. Some were smoking grass. It was mainly drinking wine or hard booze and stuff like that. We got off on that trip.

Do you have any idea of how drugs really got introduced in to the area?

Yeah. I think… this is very interesting. I think when the gangs were organized, really doing well, were going along, the leadership was really against dope. When the leadership left and the gangs started busting up, the gang members went back to their old situations of not knowing what to do. Their old frustrations came back. They had nobody to talk to. This is a direct market for dope, a direct follow-up. Some people saw that and took advantage of the situation. It then just picked up naturally. You know, when people are fucked up, they need something to do with their lives, I guess. And the whole social atmosphere of the Lower East Side was changing. It really fucked a lot of people up to know that their people were going to jail. The dope was beginning to be pushed a lot at the time. It was getting some resistance. But as the resistance went down dope got more in, and that's what happened.

Did you know about the situation while you were away or was this a total surprise?

We knew about it because we began to get guys in jail that were dope addicts who were formerly in the gangs.

What were your reactions to people you knew who now were strung out?

Well, it varied. It was very emotional. It was really a drag to know that people who had a lot going for them... one of my best friends, man... in the gangs he was really the top lieutenant... he started messing around, and when it gets as personal as that you get kinda fucked up yourself. I had to deal with it by trying to be able to influence people, while they were in jail, that when they get out not to fuck around with dope. It was like, really hard, man, because I didn't know what was out there... there was nothing else to give them then but just talking to them. I didn't know what was really out there for them to get involved with so they wouldn't have to get back into dope. So to a certain degree, it was just like talking into air. You have a situation that you're dealing with but you can't be effective on the follow-up. So I just had to deal with it as much as possible within the limits that I could.

All I could do was talk to people and try to develop an atmosphere, as much as I could, so people would tell a guy to go out and work, try to do his best. Beyond that, I really didn't know what to do. When I got out, I got a job working in a factory. That was like, the conventional thing to do. You know, stay out of trouble, get a good job. I didn't want to go back to jail. I felt bad. Okay, I went to jail. I'm out and I learned a lot from it but I didn't think it'd be too wise to get into a situation where I would have to go back again. So, at that time, the only thing I saw was getting a job. I was pretty disgusted with it because the job was pretty fucked up. And then, I don't know what happened... something happened. I just decided to stop working in that type of oppressive atmosphere and looked to see what it is that one could do. It was like really the last straw. There has to be something you can do regardless of your situation. It can't be that bad that something can't be done about it. I started talking to Chino and we got together and thought as positively as possible, trying to exclude the negative things. When mistakes did happen, we decided not to look at them so much as mistakes but learning experiences. And step-by-step-by-step and piece-by-piece, that old trick, and getting drunk enough to forget about stuff, things finally started rolling a little bit. We tried one thing. The idea of developing an army of ex-cons and ex-gang leaders and saving Cuba from Castro.

This was still in 64?

Yeah!

Wasn't that a bit of a fantasy trip?

Not really. Chino was involved with... he knew a lot of people involved with gun-running in the past. You know, for us to get guns to do what we had to do back then. There was a whole lot more where that came from. It might have been like semi-fantasy but at the time it was really realistic and we were really serious about it because we were all good fighters. We survived a lot of stuff down there. We felt we had to make ourselves acceptable to society as people rather than the animals we were before. But, really, we were fucked up at the time, thinking we could do that. We didn't realize it then, though. That just goes to show how fucked up society is to give us the idea that being big shots meant you have to shoot people and stuff like that. That's really something great. To think becoming important meant killing other people. We thought that was really great. We were really serious about it and we really talked to people about it and got other people that could actually do it... go out to Miami and organize from there.

So you were making semi-official contracts.

Right!

Did you actually make any U.S. government contracts?

No, like we were going to do that. That was like, our next step, you know, having the government support or train us. A lot of our friends were getting out of the service. They were in the Green Berets, Marine Corps Recon group. Like, really heavy fighting outfits, real fighters, they wouldn't get into nothing else but the best. So we told them, hey, you guys could train us. Get your commanding officers or somebody to get you guys detached to our group and, like, do a whole trip. They said, yeah, that's groovy. That's what they wanted to do.

For how long were you involved in this activity?

A few months, not too long, but a lot of things happened in that few months' period. From there, we met a lot of people, people who thought we were fucked up for thinking that and people who thought that it was a great idea. One thing led to another where we finally said we gotta stop this because this is not the way to do it. That's when Charlie Slack came into the picture, also.

What was that change?

I don't know what it was specifically, other than the fact that maybe we just thought that wasn't the thing to do. Maybe it was... a combination of things... getting involved in something that big showed us there are a lot of things you need to know. So you have to educate yourself. Then education really became a big thing, you know, self-education and that whole thing. Then we said maybe we better concentrate on education ourselves so we can educate others. One thing led to another. We were always independent so when we thought about education we said it'd have to be an independent-type educational system as opposed to a conventional one. No matter what you're talking about, they didn't do it for us. We asked ourselves why doesn't the conventional whole school system work. You start looking at things and really see how many other things really hook up with that, and how positive they are to that, and how negative they are to that, and then you react to it and one reaction started a whole lot of other reactions. And the negative action of going out and liberating Cuba, and the terrible ideas we had at that time, were really negative. But we thought they were positive. What happened was that it did spark off a lot of negative things, and made us investigate ourselves. So then that turned into a positive thing. In other words, we were able to handle good situations and bad situations, and somehow survive them all. And the main thing that kept us going was a real tightness in the group. We were really a tight group. We really knew how to deal with each other on personal levels as opposed to having a heavy argument with a guy and splitting up because of that heavy argument. Although heavy things happened, we were able somehow to control them so it was a whole basic humanistic type thing that was happening and happening right to a large part even though a lot of wrong things happen. But the basic things, the strong things were happening right and let us build on that. A strong foundation was being developed, so we built on that.

What was the next activity you embarked on?

Basically education. Like, the University of the Streets.

How did that get started?

As things kept going, different people began to hear about us and therefore feed in more ideas of different possibilities. People got hooked up with us and we took ideas and changed them around to how we felt we could deal with it, and dealt with it. That's how the University of the Streets came about.

Had you become RGS by that time?

Yeah! Right! We had become RGS, the Real Great Society, not really knowing what that fully meant but trying to get to it and trying to keep our independence. That was necessary because we didn't

143

know ourselves beyond the fact that we had to keep trying. We were people trying a lot of things. Some came out good; other things were bad. Actually, we tried to develop an independent financial base and that seemed to get into a whole heavy, conventional commercial trip, that was really like fucked up for us because we didn't want to deal with that whole thing. You have to almost change your whole life and become a different human being to have to deal on the conventional commercial level. We tried it to see if we could get it and turn it around and direct it toward what we wanted to do. It didn't turn out too good because we weren't really ready for it. There were a number of commercial ventures we tried. They worked out, and we learned a lot from them, but I think they didn't work out in the way they were supposed to work out, conventionally. But, to us, they worked out. We were able to experience the commercial trip so we knew what was happening. We learned we don't want it but we also knew that, to a certain degree, financial independence had to be dealt with. We knew two things… it was like some mathematics. We had two parts to a triangle, and the other part wasn't there yet, but we knew we needed it. We knew we didn't want to do it the conventional way, so another way had to be developed. And that was kind of the next step: what was the other way? We didn't know ourselves half the time. But, basically, whether we voiced it or not, in our minds we were heading toward that.

And you feel that the University of the Streets was really the first positive step in that direction?

I think they were all positive steps in the right direction. The University of the Streets was like a big step, it had a lot to do with people and it proved a lot of things to us. It proved that we could do something like nobody else had really done. Particularly that people like us could be expected to do something like that.

Could you tell me what is the University of the Streets?

Well, basically, I think it was a place where people could for once talk to each other, trust each other, and begin whatever it was that it takes to learn from each other. Getting away from the conventional things that only the teacher could teach. We finally really learned that every human being is like a teacher and everybody could teach something to somebody. Everybody had something about them that was really important. That got into a whole thing where conventional things that people were teaching wasn't really that important. As a matter of fact, it was a big joke to a certain degree to have to go through all this waste of time to learn things that really weren't that important for your life. Simply, being able to communicate, I think. That was really important. Simply for people, not just Puerto Ricans, but all kinds (flower kids were out at that time and that whole trip), for people being able to communicate, I think. That was really important. Some of the classes went pretty good, like the Theater of Courage, a few other things went pretty good too. A lot of people developed a lot of things out of it. It was a place where a lot of people developed... you know, found out that they had something about them.

You mentioned Charlie Slack earlier. How did he help you?

Charlie Slack used to be a kind of social work type guy back during the gang days when Chino met him. Chino used to hang out on the West Side. Charlie had some ideas that he wanted to work out with gangs about how they react to different ideas. Like, if you had money, would you still be a guy in a gang, still going around beating up people and stuff. So, he got a grant and gave people money, drove them around in limousines, flew them around in helicopters, opened up charge accounts in department stores and clothes stores and stuff like that and kept the guys busy enough so they wouldn't be committing crimes, and then he took a census from the closest police station to see how many crimes were in their district from the day he started to the day he finished. The rate of crime went down.

So that's how we met Charlie. He had a lot of far-out crazy ideas that we all thought were kinda crazy at the time. Me and Chino went to meet him. We told him some of the ideas we had about education, about just doing things. We said we're looking for a change. Some of the things we're looking for, we don't even know what they are. But we know that what we got, we don't like. So, we started rapping. Somehow we decided that we have to look beyond what was on the Lower East Side. We had to speak to a lot of people to get more ideas to be better able to find out what it is that we want. To look at the whole picture and study the whole picture. Or, as much of the whole picture as we could. What were the resources we had available?

So that's what we did. We started travelling and talking to people. People would invite us to give lectures. Out of that came meeting people who were interested in what you are all about and seeing how you're fucked up and how they're fucked up. Everybody began developing a feeling of communication. We kept in touch with the people we began to meet around the country. When they came to New York they stayed and lived with us. They stayed and worked with us. We were being invited to speak to people who wanted to start an organization similar to ours or to be able to better relate to their community. We travelled to every major city in the United States and a majority of the top universities. Also, a lot of business and foundation gatherings. It was really an excellent PR job Charlie Slack had during those trips.

It kind of built us up. It also helped us find out where a lot of people were at. We found out where the country itself was at, the whole thing. We found out where we were at. Out of that, we were able to build up our own picture of how we saw things.

How did you come across Buckminster Fuller?

That happened with Fred Good. He read more than we did. He had heard of Bucky somehow through his travels and I guess he thought it would be a good idea to hook up together. I found a lot of things happening. One person would know another person and say well, if these people got together, maybe something could come out of it. A lot of times it did and a lot of time it didn't. This is how we met Bucky.

Do you remember when this meeting was?

It was maybe about March 1968. Bucky got up on the stage of this meeting hall across Tompkins Square Park from the University of the Streets headquarters. He was supposedly coming in to tell us what to do and people got really turned off by him. A lot of people were into strong "only brother" trips. They didn't trust the white world. Chino got up on stage and told everybody to shut the hell up and listen to what the guy was saying. Then they liked what he was saying. The people started listening. We later talked to Bucky when he was eating his steak meal. From there on in, we became friends. We started keeping in touch with each other. The thing about the domes didn't come up until about two years later, at least. A long time after Bucky came down.

What was the transition from the RGS group into the CHARAS situation?

Well, a lot of things. RGS developed almost into a superstructure, like a really big organization, really a lot of people. Sometimes the really important things weren't getting done, like one being able to communicate with somebody else, really communicate. Things got so tied up into red tape.

Administration?

Yeah! Administration, dealing with government and dealing with people all around the country and businessmen. They wasted all our time. We were duplicating what was happening in the outside society, so we decided to start CHARAS.

When did this decision first occur?

I don't remember specifically. I just remember... it was just something that developed in our minds. First of all, Chino and myself came up with the idea that we wanted to like turn it over to other people and go on to something else. We felt that it's better that way. You know, start something, reinforce it as much as possible and let other people do it, then see what else you can get into. We'd say ok, this is happening. Some people are benefiting, some people are not bene-fiting. But it's happening. Other people could take it from here. We learned a lot from it. We met a lot of people. Maybe other stuff should start happening. The idea was enforced when the RGS organization got bigger and as things got more administratively restricted. We said, let's completely stop this and start something else.

What year was it when you began feeling that?

Probably in 68 when we started having a lot of money. We had lots of money and lots of programs and stuff like that and we said, oh! To a certain degree our job is done here, move on and do something else… and then we started deciding. There was a whole social thing going on. Everybody was into the poverty game. Everybody trying to hustle the government and it started to become a joke. We said, hey, a lot of people are getting turned off by this. Particularly people who hadn't been able to achieve anything. With all the programs that were going on, there were still people that… just got turned off by the whole thing.

Let's try to do something, we said, with people who never had been involved with social groups or don't even know what's happen-ing. That's how we developed CHARAS. Roy and Crespo and a few of the other fellows were not involved with RGS. Or if they were involved, they didn't dig it and were looking for a change also. That's how we developed it. We'd say, listen man, what's happening is fucked up, let's not continue doing fucked up things, let's try to do something… use what we learned as a tool to be able to get into something else. We don't have to be so controlled. That's what happened in RGS. It became controlled by a lot of conventional things which didn't leave it enough time to be creatively working within the system, but construc-tively. So that was what we decided. Everybody agreed. But nobody really knew what to do.

And when did you call Bucky again?

Around the end of 69 or the beginning of 70. We got on that because we had a pretty heavy housing program going on in East Harlem with Puerto Rican architects who got out of school and came back to the community and were doing some pretty heavy things. We looked at housing as something very important. Living in a place, it means a whole lot more than just living in a place. It means a whole social atmosphere. It means, to a large degree, one's education, real education. It means being able to handle, to cope with the immediate situation and try to relate back to the overall because it comes from the house. Ok, you're not satisfied with the house, you don't own the house, you live in shitty houses and because you live in shitty houses everything else happens after that, you know. How you relate to people. How people relate to you. How you feel funny if you go into a rich neighborhood. So we thought that housing was basic. At one point in time, the only one we knew that was doing something extremely different and made sense was Bucky. But we first had to know if we really could live with each other. Could we go through a real experience, and how would we come out of it. If this could be accomplished, let's sit down and talk about what's the next step, if there is a next step.

And that's how you got into the Outward Bound Program?

Right! You see, originally, I got into the Outward Bound program on my own because things were getting like so fucked up over here and I had to get away and it just wasn't a regular type of getting away. It was really a heavy-duty experience, enough to snap me out of what I was doing.

How would you describe Outward Bound?

I would describe it really as my master's degree, in like a bit of sociology, a bit of human relations, and a bit of knowing myself a whole lot better than I did before that.

What specifically is it?

Outward Bound is a survival school, an outdoor survival school. You learn how to survive in the outdoors and also how to come into a situation with a group of people that you never knew before and after thirty days that group of people is still together and you've accomplished what—if you would have thought about it before—would almost seem impossible. Example: going out in the rough sea in a whale boat with about fifteen people. That whale boat was really cramped up. It was a real life situation. If something wasn't done fast, you would get killed, like running into a lot of reefs or somebody falling overboard. You have to learn how to talk to each other. You have to develop who's able to do what best, really fast. You have to develop all of the basic life survival skills—with people who you've never known before from all walks of life. We did it somehow. Nobody got hurt, we did it, and there were a lot of those situations that continually happened. A real life thing where each person is building up all of his creativeness, his energy, his pride, everything that he has to deal with in real life situations.

So when we joined Outward Bound we went to Colorado and Mexico with a medical team to help Mexican Indians. I really went through a lot of changes because my wife was having a child and I had to really make a decision as to be with my wife or to get involved in what I really believed in at the time. A really big decision. I decided to continue what I had started and hoped my wife would understand that my baby was also important to me. But this was also important to me and like, I was really doing it for my children. I hoped that she would realize that. But, she didn't. Decisions like that had to be made. It was that real, and it still is. It gets more heavy, and to be able to face all the things that go on every day, to stop things because you have no choice and to be able to continue, go the next step, whatever the next step is. Sometimes there is no next step.

So you think if every human being has intelligence and resources and enough backbone, you could do it. You begin. You can develop it. You can become involved in what you really want to do, what's important to you as an individual, and begin to realize and appreciate the real values of life. The value of another human being to another. The value of being able to communicate to another person. Yet not get it so complex that you can't deal with it. Being able to get away from what society says you can't do. That was the whole trip of Mike Ben-Eli coming in and teaching us how to build domes. People actually learned how to build domes. It was following up theory with experience. First, you think what you're gonna do and then follow it up and physically experience it. I think that's basically what it's all about. It can't be all theory, or all experience. It has to be a combination of both.

Angelo, other than seeing CHARAS as a dome-building operation and an experience in which people could deal with one another on a humanistic basis, what else do you see as a philosophic objective in CHARAS?

I see it as an energy force. An energy force that's out there for people to use. Some are using it and some are not using it. I see it as something that proves that something can be done at any time. We're trying to say that you can think about doing something, want to do something, and then actually do it. It's like another tool that's out there. A tool that could be used at all times. It's an energy force or tool that can grow bigger if it wants to and can be directed off into a lot of other things. Or, it could stay the way it is and still be an energy force that people could always look back on, knowing that something is happening like... the Real Great Society.

And draw from it?

And draw from it, right!

What do you see for tomorrow?

Only that more things could happen. I see that. I don't know how. I'm excited about life. Once in a while you get negative about it, but tomorrow is another chance to continue what you're doing and develop new ways. Tomorrow is tomorrow. It's very simplistic. It's like a continuation of what you're doing now, I guess. And the hope to be able to continue, the hope to be able to see what you're doing, and the knowledge that you could change what you're doing now.

It's like an open channel...

Right, exactly. You know something else could happen. No more, no less. It could happen if you want it to. Or it could just be another day and you don't do anything. Either way.

Angelo had been talking for nearly an hour and a half. His voice was now sounding totally graveled. Angelo's head cold had now watered his eyes. His nose had turned very red from the constant blowing and dabbing. Although the room was very cold, his T-shirt was streaked with perspiration.

Falling back onto the bed, Angelo let out a howl of relief. The tension of uprooting his past and thinking as intently as he had, plus the discomfort of his cold, made him hunch into himself. He then stretched his paunchy body toward the ceiling, sprang up, and called out to Evelyn for something to eat. She shouted back that her mother had prepared a Puerto Rican country-style chicken.

There was no conversation while Angelo ate. When he finished, Evelyn asked when they were leaving for the farm. He grumbled something about maybe later in the afternoon or early the next morning. Pushing himself away from the table, he started for the front door, grabbing his jacket from the back of the kitchen chair. Evelyn asked him to bring back cigarettes. He looked back at her, promising that he would.

While he was waiting for the elevator, Evelyn opened the apartment door and, very apprehensively, asked when he was returning. "When I get back just be ready to leave," he said as the elevator door opened.

He found the borrowed pick-up truck and quickly pulled out of the parking space, heading west on Delancy Street. At the Essex Street subway entrance, he stopped and said, "Yeah, I said a lot, didn't I? I'll have to think about it again. Maybe I'll learn something new."

The pick-up truck was soon lost in the rapidly moving traffic.

Angelo Gonzalez, Jr.

The Original Six

Roy Battiste

"I'm probably the most knowledgeable person regarding domes at CHARAS. So naturally, information is power. But I don't consider myself a leader." Roy says this with an expressionless face as he sits on the convertible sofa bed that is covered by an American flag. This is one of the first of many facets that become apparent in Roy Battiste.

When Chino and Angelo asked Roy to join them in the formation of the group to be dubbed CHARAS, they must have known, consciously or subliminally, that Roy would be most receptive to the abstract dome concepts. He would, thereby, be able to help and lead any and all that were to join them in their venture.

The loft at 303 Cherry Street is both home and work area for Roy. It represents him and serves his lifestyle. The third-story loft, in the soon-to-be-demolished city-owned building, is 50' by 50'. It is divided into a kitchen, an office, two large sleeping areas, a living room space, and a general open space. This description of the loft interior is actually inadequate to convey its impact. You first pound on the door, are admitted, greeted by Roy's German Shepherd (named Sabu), get accustomed to the dimly lit entrance area, and then you become suddenly aware of two unexpected sights. Ahead of you and to your left is a black-lighted wall mural of comic-book style futuristic galactic space. Further on the left you see a white duck-cloth dome structure approximately 18' in diameter. Between this dome and the wall with the mural is the kitchen area. The conventional kitchen nestling next to the dome structure creates an interesting ambiance of contrasts.

This first dome houses the private space Luis Lopez created for himself from the duck cloth and discarded lumber two-by-fours to form the triangular geodesic form. The entire structure cost about $25.00. It provides the sleep and private work area Luis needs.

Beyond this dome, making a sharp right, you are in the office and work area. There are tools hung on the far right wall. A desk and work table laden with books and papers flank this wall. Down towards the windows is the drafting table and equipment. In this long corridor filled with the essentials of organizational and technical paraphernalia, on your left you suddenly become aware of an old-fashioned office wooden partition that acts as a wall support for another cloth dome area. The area is divided into two sections: a sitting space filled with stereo equipment, speakers, bookshelves, a couch, several chairs, and dome models hung from various supports; and another with the flag-draped sofa, an old television set, a chair, low storage chests, and a brightly lit fish tank filled with exotic species.

Each individual area has a sense of intimacy, warmth, hand-me-down comfort and a quality of unhurried life patterns—as does the entire loft. To the casual Lower East Side visitor, the loft is an incredible experience. Here, space and objects are devoted to an expression of personal development and fulfillment unknown in their project or tenement apartments. To the more sophisticated visitor, this space becomes the unique solving of interesting space problems and an expression of a definite lifestyle and outlook. What either visitor is not aware of is the fact that there is no hot water, poor heat in winter and no bathing facilities. So though it may look clean, cozy, affable and inviting, living here does present problems.

Roy's presence and interests dominate this space. It may be the official address for CHARAS but it is decidedly Roy's home and work space. This is evident only by indirection but it is evident.

Roy is a twenty-nine-year-old Puerto Rican born in the Virgin Islands and brought to New York's Spanish Harlem when he was two. He appears at times to be inwardly distracted. His receding hairline offers his compact facial features a sense of release. Depending upon his mood, Roy sports a neat beard or is clean shaven. You usually have to strain to hear his soft, resonant, unaccented voice. He may have sleep drenched eyes but, without advance warning, they will become very keen and piercing.

There is much in his background that has made him cynical. His infrequent retreats into silence or non-participation have deep roots in his struggle to survive. He learned to be a loner early in his life as an escape from many of the disgusting aspects of his environment. There is an unexpressed rage in Roy at the injustices he has experienced, witnessed and known to have existed around him. He appears to be a concerned person but is seemingly unmoved by having had one brother seriously injured and another brother actually die because of junk. His growth from early youth to young manhood has been a constant series of reassessments. His involvement and development in CHARAS may have led him toward positive actions. Without CHARAS, his instincts and intuitions indicated that he might have followed other, more negative directions.

By the time Roy was in junior high school, his family had moved to the Lower East Side. He enjoyed school. He didn't get into any trouble. He was surrounded with gangs in his youth but had little to do with them except for sporadic friendships. The gang members considered him a "book worm" and felt he was "cool." He moved easily, therefore, from gang to gang without any hindrance or involvement.

After his graduation from Haaren High School he went on to college for a short sprint. He didn't like college and soon quit. Entering the Air Force, thereafter, he was to remain for two and one half years. When asked why he chose the Air Force over any other branch of the armed forces, he responds characteristically with "They're all the same bullshit."

In the Air Force Roy was trained to work with a motion picture support squadron at a missile base in California. He received security clearance for this work and settled in to do his tour. The Air Force and Roy did not get along all the time.

Roy, quietly, relates his experiences in the Air Force with a detachment and lack of interest one displays towards an unremembered meal of the previous day. "There's no room for individuality in the military. I'm a heavy individual and I didn't like the lack of freedom." He arranged to get himself "divorced" from the Air Force after two and one half years. He never mentions how this was done. The important thing is tht he got out. He then came home to New York and merely hung out for nearly a year. Chino and Angelo were already talking to people about a new set of circumstances for their life on the Lower East Side and life in general. Roy listened but did not know yet if he wanted to join or contribute in any way.

"I wanted to travel," Roy says. "I wanted to experience something more than New York, you know." He then quickly recounts the next two years: living in California and working in computer repair for IBM. He finally had it with the California scene and had himself transferred by IBM to New York where he worked another two years. During this period, he had his own apartment in the Longfellow section of the Southeast Bronx. He would see his friends on the Lower East Side occasionally. On these weekends he would "party" with them and goof away the time. The turning point for him began to occur when the social conditions of his job became openly abhorrent. "I began to see that IBM was just a lot of bullshit. And where I was living up in the Bronx, I was watching dope coming in and seeing people change. I began seeing crime go up. I began to wonder what I could do about all this. Working at IBM just didn't give me any kind of satisfaction. I didn't feel I was doing anything for anybody other than IBM."

The layers of contradiction and concern in Roy were beginning to unfold. He didn't know what he wanted to do. He just knew what he was doing was not doing any good in directions he began feeling were important and significant.

As Roy continues relating the chronology of these events, a greater sense of interest and urgency are evident in his voice and eyes. His body, very slouched on the sofa before, is now alert and seated upright. It is obvious that the past is of little interest to Roy. Relating the autobiography was a painful chore for him. His concerns are with the present and with shaping an aspect of tomorrow. As he goes on telling his story, he now allows a laugh of a remembered incident to escape, contrasted with the previous tight-guardedness.

"Well, I quit IBM. I sort of hung out with everybody for a while. Then I sort of drifted by myself for a while. In early 70 Chino and Angelo asked me to get involved with a program dealing with housing. I thought about it for a little while and it seemed interesting. That's when we started with CHARAS."

It was Angelo who suggested that this new group of six join an Outward Bound expedition. Roy remembers it as "a demonstration of sincerity, fortitude or whatever." In January, 1970, they were all off to Mexico as a medical assistance unit with Outward Bound. When they returned in March, classes with Michael Ben-Eli commenced. A whole new chapter of Roy's growth and discovery was now initiated.

Most of the people involved with CHARAS were street people. They lived most of their youth "hanging out" on the streets of their neighborhoods. The physical and spiritual conditions of their homes were such that the street, with their peers as equal victims or victors, offered a more congenial atmosphere. Roy had been around these people all his life although he had not fully participated in their activities. But he understood their mores and conditions. He understood that most of the events these people had experienced at home, school, on the job, etc. had been primarily negative. They were, therefore, conditioned to failure and social abuse.

The young men who joined together to form CHARAS had all had the same backgrounds. The usual teacher-student role would never function successfully with these people. They were turned off to this circumstance that had only negative memories for them. The first "teacher" Bucky had sent to CHARAS had not been able to cope with the group and left without any visible results. When Michael joined the CHARAS group in March 1970, he was also to have a long and difficult time with them. He, fortunately, was as willing to learn from them as he was eager to teach them. He learned to be patient and to stimulate their imagination and intelligence. They learned the skills of dome building. Roy was particularly proficient in absorbing the complex and abstract ideas related to geodesic domes. What was also happening of equal worth was a group dynamic based on commonality of experience and goal.

The period between 1970 to 1972 was one of continuous struggle and growth. Several of the original members of CHARAS became involved with other activities (due to personal pressures or newly developed interests) but Roy held on to his interest and purpose.

Michael was a continual feeder of information and training to Roy and whoever else showed interest.

Roy had been able, during this period, to interest and attract a new flow of people who came to the loft to learn and work. Some came to live at the loft. This produced new experiences with which to deal. In his quixotic manner, Roy assembled a new generation of CHARAS participants who considered the loft on Cherry Street a vibrant part of their young lives.

CHARAS proceeded from severe struggle to moderate grappling with survival. The help of the New York State Council on the Arts, finally helped. But what was developing with the inner fabric of CHARAS was the most significant. All the people who worked with CHARAS, either living there or occasionally visiting, developed a cooperative attitude dedicated to the continued growth and success of CHARAS. They helped with money for food and other bills. They gave of their time and energies on the various projects at the School of Visual Arts, Ruppert Brewery site, exhibitions at conferences and the general maintenance of the loft and newly acquired fourth-floor building workshop. There was a general feeling of purpose that grew. This became the important element that Roy saw developing around him through the activities he quietly directed.

If asked what may be an overriding philosophy operating at CHARAS, Roy will at first scoff at the idea and deny there is one. But if he is pressed, he leans back on his sofa and his eyes begin seriously watching his fish swim about mysteriously in their tank enclosure. After some measurable pause he begins speaking very slowly and carefully.

"I see it primarily as educational. But a more dynamic kind of education. An education that allowed people to learn something new that they could use to help people who have little means. Colleges are supposed to do that. They train people who then are supposed to go out and do something for others. Mostly they do things for themselves. We try to do the same thing even if it only broadens the way they look at things.

"You just can't think about yourself. You have to think about other people too because your life is dependent on what happens to other people in the world. If there are poor people in the world then you're poor too. And you have to fight to overcome that.

"I would hope that we would be able to demonstrate to people that it is possible to do something. Most people feel there isn't anything that they can do. Our program shows we've been able to accomplish what we have with very few resources. Now we serve as an inspiration to other people.

"I would hope that we would really be able to get into experimenting with different housing structures and building them for people. Maybe we'll try to get business involved in a really constructive kind of way. We're not looking for a commercial relationship. But, maybe, the way we can do it in cooperation with business and government. They can support the research and development of what we do and adapt it for larger use. A lot of people come up here and they see the loft and think it costs lots of money to put it together. When we tell them how we did it, it gets them thinking what they can do for themselves.

"I'd just like to become a little more proficient at helping people."

Roy settles into the sofa cushions and lapses into a silence. The quality of paradox cloaks him again. He seemingly retreats, looks back at the fish tank. He seems to be trying to communicate with them as he is trying to communicate with those around him. But he has also learned that you win a few and you lose a few. Nevertheless, you keep trying and that is what Roy is all about.

Moses Anthony Figueroa

Moses Anthony Figueroa beams a bright flashing smile as he states, "My hobby is thinking." He now lives in the upper northern section of Manhattan. The three-room apartment is far from the gang-infested youth he knew in Brooklyn or the troubled years of discovery spent on the Lower East Side.

At 30, Moses is a handsome, quick-talking, eclectic person whose early background reads like a litany of the streets. But now, surrounded by his original comic book drawings, bits of movie film strips, and notebooks of writing, it is difficult to imagine Moses living through the danger, horror, ignominy, and emotional complexity of his youth.

"My story is a very strange story," Moses plunges right in. He speaks easily, with clarity and confidence. "There was a power play in my family for me. So, like, I have brothers that I know very well but they're not really my brothers. I was raised alone. It's one of those tragic cases." Without rancor or bitterness, he tells stories of his past which detail every form of neglect, privation, and suffering. He has been able to see his past for what it was and views it as a lesson not to be repeated.

"You know, my father was a revolutionary in Puerto Rico. He advocated the liberation of Puerto Rico as an independent state allied with the United States. It's a dream that I share with my father. Unfortunately, now, he is very old and his mind is full of religion." Moses goes on to explain that his father was forty-seven and his mother was sixteen when he was born. With pride glowing from his dark eyes, Moses declares, "And my mother's an Indian. The area where my mother grew up is far away from the main hub of the city, next to the beach and a river. I had the privilege of getting to know my great-grandmother." Moses did not get to know his mother until his early teen years. He was given over to an aunt with whom he lived until he was five. The aunt was a local doctor in Puerto Rico.

She encouraged Moses' intellectual pursuits at this very early age. By the time Moses moved to the Bay Ridge section of Brooklyn, to join his father, he was able to read and write Spanish fluently and had acquired some knowledge of English.

The local school in which Moses was enrolled was soon baffled by his ability. He was alternately promoted and demoted in his school ranking. At one time he was placed in a class for retarded children because his English was not on par with the other New York-born classmates. His entire elementary-school period was fraught with confusion and resentment. Being Puerto Rican had become a stigma. He soon learned that to be different had a heavy price.

The neighborhood to which he first moved was basically

composed of people whose backgrounds were Irish, Italian, and German. A young boy from Puerto Rico was an oddity. The difficulties he was facing in school spilled out onto the street. Moses was constantly assaulted by various neighborhood bullies all through his elementary and junior high school years. He had no one to share this with at home since his father worked all night and slept all day. The only solution Moses had was to retreat from the dangers of the street. He would remain at home, after school, devouring comic books and watching television from six to ten hours a day.

"So, school was not fulfilling me," Moses says as he stretches out on his make-shift couch in the work room he has established in his apartment. The faulty air conditioner is trying to dispel the early June humid air. The walls are covered with comic book posters Moses has drawn and collected. The rom has a good feeling about it. A sense of creative energy vibrates within this room. He continues, "My home life was not fulfilling also. I lived with a man who was already old. There was a forty-year gap between us. Because he worked at night, and did not leave the house until 5PM, he didn't want me in the house because I made too much noise. So after my father would leave, instead of going outside and getting cold and getting myself into trouble, I would stay in and watch television. All the time I would get myself into trouble in the streets, and guys hunted you down. If you go into the streets you've got to be jumping from alley to alley until you can get to a safe turf where nobody will hunt you down, but to me that was a drag."

Moses' basic curiosity, nurtured by his reading of fantastical comic books, made his television viewing somewhat more selective. "I hated comedy shows," Moses states. "I always liked educational programs like *In Search of Ancient Astronauts*. So all my life I've been fighting for a little liberty so I could just think. I love thinking. I like to just sit around and think about things."

But whenever Moses ventured out of his environs, he discovered he had to defend himself. He quickly learned who the few other young Puerto Rican boys were and they banded together to protect themselves from the hostile neighborhood youths. This involvement began when Moses was nearly ten years old and continued for the next seven years of his life, with occasional lapses. His intricate activities within the gang structure ranged from simple participation to "war lord" positions. Over these years, Moses found himself involved in open battle with rival gangs and the police. At one interval, Moses became the shadow (personal runner) for a rising member of the Puerto Rican criminal world. In many ways, this man became the surrogate father Moses needed and had not found in the relationship with his father.

While in junior high school, dope began to enter Moses' life. "We were skin-popping it," Moses says in a voice touched with sadness. "But we used it for a different purpose in those days. We didn't use it to blow our skulls. We used it because it made us more powerful. I remember working myself up and skin popping and going out for a rumble. After a while, you started riding the 'H' and some of the guys got hooked on it and got completely fucked up. I was lucky and saw what I did. I had this inbuilt desire for freedom. I can't let myself be in an undignified position. But dope did trap me. It made me hesitant about things.

"I have seen guys mainline and go insane. And I was afraid, so I tried not to mainline. But I knew that I was caught by something that was threatening something inside me and I knew that I had to fight. I must have gone out of my skull at this time. So, my father shipped me off to Puerto Rico."

Moses then relates the difficulty of trying to adjust to a foreign situation while going through the symptoms of "cold turkey." Conditions became severe. The pressure he felt culminated in one day of mayhem when he ripped his classroom apart, throwing desks and chairs out the window. He also threw a teacher down a flight of stairs. Obviously, Moses was dismissed from school. He then began a trek across the island, looking for the village in which his mother and family lived.

During this period, Moses discovered the deep roots he had for the Puerto Rican island and people. He roamed all over, absorbing the wonder and beauty of the land and the warmth and simple truth of the people he encountered. Moses then fell into a situation that most young boys dream about but few experience. He chanced upon a carnival travelling through the countryside of Puerto Rico.

The combination of working at the carnival and the eventual discovery of his mother and family had a profound impact on Moses. For the first time in his life, he felt a sense of belonging and fulfillment. These situations began to erase the ugliness and sordidness of his life in New York City. A deeper feeling of the true meaning of a tranquil life gave him a viable alternate to the chaos of his personal and environmental existence.

Moses was in Puerto Rico for nearly nine months before returning to his father in New York City. He then discovered that his father was living in the Jamaica section of Queens. Mr. Figueroa was sharing the home of a relative, a policeman who had a son Moses' age. The relative was stern in his dealings with the two boys. Moses' father was of little influence since he had become a nearly hopeless alcoholic.

Moses then enrolled in Jamaica High School. He enjoyed school because his intellectual abilities were being tested and appreciated. Moses' father was unable to adequately support his basic needs for clothing and pocket money. This caused great anxiety. He sadly relates "Now here I come, with my little brown skin and my cousin. Now, all I had was a pair of black chino pants and cowboy boots, and a cowboy shirt with stripes and a cowboy hat I used to wear. At that time I was called 'Tex.'"

Moses discovered that the rest of the school was decidedly middle-class in dress, demeanor, available money, and outlook. According to Moses, his cousin, Tonito, was not very bright. He was big and hulking. The two must have been quite a duo in this basically white school situation.

Moses escaped every weekend to his old friends back in Brooklyn. They would party and get drunk. He would then return to the frustration of his home and school. At this time Moses discovered he liked to write short stories. But he received no recognition or acknowledgement for his efforts. This increased his hostility and led to constant fighting with other students. He found himself in an enveloping circle of frustration and discrimination. When his father was informed of Moses' negative behavior at school, he would accuse him of being a 'troublemaker,' causing his son to react with further antagonistic patterns. Conditions grew more intense until finally Moses was sent away to reform school. "This was a very vague period in my life," Moses states. "There are things I can't even remember. There are many periods in my life I haven't been able to put together."

By some fortunate stroke of luck, Moses was placed on the swimming team during his second semester and became a valued member of the team. His troubles subsided during this period. Moses applied himself and discovered a new sense of contentment. This was short lived, however. His father decided to move back to Brooklyn. He moved into a low-income project in the Brownsville section. When the Jamaica High School authorities discovered he no longer lived in their school district, Moses was dismissed. He fell into a state of gloom.

"So, they turned me over to Thomas Jefferson High School in Brooklyn and from there I got transferred to about nine other schools, and I just couldn't get along in the other schools, because people tried to abuse me, and I wouldn't let them." Moses was now floating without any purpose or direction. Whatever positive patterns he had learned to appreciate and cherish were now non-existent. He was aimless and angry.

Moses found himself back in the gang life in Brownsville. But this time the gangs didn't fool around with fist fights or garrison belts. The era of the hand-made gun had arrived. Some actually had the real thing. Gang war was now very real. Neighborhoods became battle grounds. Rooftops were sniper hideouts and Molotov cocktail launching pads. Wandering into other gang's territory could result in instant death.

Two young women in this neighborhood probably saved his life. The first got him to withdraw from active gang participation. Later, the other one interested Moses in the Methodist Evangelical Church. Moses became very active in the choral group and began travelling around the city performing at different churches. The rest of the city now became known to him. His insularity was now replaced by new dimensions with this extension of his life.

He then went into a series of jobs at various Manhattan advertising agencies, assisting in the departments. He was also trying to accomplish an ongoing dream: to work with a comic strip artist. He was not successful at this desire. But, to his great surprise, in 1962 he fell in with a theatric crowd and chanced upon a summer stock job in *West Side Story*. Again Moses' irascibility, unfortunately, got him fired just before the opening of the musical.

Thereafter, Moses drifted in and out of jobs and events that had little meaning or significance. Finally, in 1964, a distant relative suggest Moses become a gardener for a middle-income co-op housing complex. He applied and was accepted. Moses spent the year moving from housing project to housing project because of his concern with the plight of the workers and their exploitation by both the management and the union. He was soon edged out of employment.

In 1965, Moses decided it was really time for him to try developing his interest in comic strip writing and drawing. He arduously wrote seven complete comic strips and attempted to sell them within the comic book industry. Moses could not crack through. He then decided to go back to advertising art and, after many unsuccessful forays, landed a job with Pace Advertising agency. He began as a file clerk. He also did some art production work. He was earning $70.00 per week for both assignments. His industry and energy soon promoted him to an assistantship to a top person in production. He adapted well, and did his job with efficiency and ease.

Each request for an increase in salary went unanswered. At one point, Moses was slipped a five-dollar increase as a token gesture. Needing the money, Moses accepted this but realized his demeaning position. One day he just stayed home, refusing all entreaties to come back to work. He was finally offered an additional five dollars, and returned, begrudgingly, to Pace. Everything was decidedly downhill from that point on.

Moses left Pace and sought work at other advertising agencies. Nothing was happening. He had developed what he thought was a dynamite new comic book portfolio which he now brought to the comic book agencies. There was no opportunity offered. His frustration began to grow. After one fruitless episode, Moses found himself walking down the streets of mid-Manhattan actually hitting passersby. It had begun to rain. His neat "Madison Avenue" grooming was becoming disheveled as he raced down the street hitting out, being hit, and falling down. The police finally arrived while he was being held down by one of the men he had struck. One of the police officers recognized Moses' disorientation. He sat Moses in the patrol car and talked to him. The officer explained that if he booked Moses, the courts might not understand the inner stresses of his situation. He suggested that they go to Bellevue Hospital and have Moses place himself under psychiatric observation.

Moses is not quite sure of the time he spent in Bellevue. He estimates he was there for two months. For a short period, he was in an experimental section used for various drug medication tests. Noticing strange behavior changes in one of the patients on this ward, Moses forced himself back to the first section into which he was admitted. Although his mind had snapped, his will to survive was as active as it had ever been.

As a result of an inadvertent comment made by his father, the doctors at Bellevue determined that Moses must be assigned to Pilgrim State Hospital on Long Island. Moses discovered that Pilgrim was not a very cool place to be. Using some knowledge gained from the wards, he managed to get transferred to Central Islip Hospital further out on Long Island.

The next two and a half years are very vague in Moses' recollection. The time spent between Bellevue and Central Islip, which are principally blank in his memory, he used as positively as possible. He attempted to read and draw as much as his non-doped consciousness allowed. His immediate attendants did not appreciate his independent attitude. Even here, Moses was encountering the excessive pressures of a controlling societal force thwarting his natural impulses and instincts.

Because of the many adverse experiences Moses underwent during his incarceration at Central Islip Hospital, a healthy disrespect for psychiatry and social workers developed that lasts to this day. Moses contends, "You can't tell me the very people that are taking care of your head and set the laws for you aren't the same people who have the highest rate of suicide of any professional group." His bitterness and resentment is vibrant towards this entire period. As with no other time in his life, Moses feels he did not gain or learn from these events. The waste of energy and the length of vacuity still gnaw at him.

When Moses was finally released from the mental hospital sometime in 1967, he returned to his earlier effort to enter the world of comic book drawing and writing. He developed new concepts and formulas. But, again, he found his efforts to be of no avail. Finally, needing employment, he became a messenger with a service on 45th Street. The return to a "nothing" job was debilitating. When he went to his old neighborhood in Brooklyn, the scene he discovered there displeased him greatly. Most of the young men he had known within the gang structure were now into drugs or heavy criminal activities. Both of these paths had little interest for Moses.

In his drifting and searching for a base, Moses discovered a mental rehabilitation halfway house organization called Fountain House. He became active in the program, out of a need for a place to live and adjust to his new circumstances. "But I couldn't conform to what they wanted," Moses recalls, "and, finally, I revolted and had all of the others join me in organizing ourselves so that we could determine our existence inside the Fountain House institution. What they (Fountain House) actually did was, being a private charity with government support, they were supposed to rehabilitate mental patients. But what they really did was make the patients go crazy so that they could forever claim them." Moses soon departed with no regrets to anyone.

A short excursion with the radical Young Lords of Spanish Harlem then followed. "But we just couldn't hit it off," says Moses. "Their philosophy and my philosophy were just too different from each other. Consequently, they saw me as a threat rather than as an ally." He became further disenchanted when he was at a rooftop meeting on 5th street on the Lower East Side. The Young Lords had invited a member of the Students for a Democratic Society to discuss techniques of guerilla warfare. When Moses proposed some other alternatives, they turned on him and demanded to know where the money for his ideas were going to come from. Incensed, Moses relates, "I didn't have to take this shit from the Young Lords or any other Puerto Ricans. If I didn't take shit from those people in the mental hospital, then, definitely, I wasn't going to take it from my own people."

The only positive outcome from Moses' skirmish with the Young Lords was an introduction to Chino Garcia. Chino, through the Real Great Society, was conducting serious discussions with the Young

Lords and participating in some community-related programs that benefited the aims of both groups.

"Then one day at the end of 1968, I just walked into Chino's office. I said, this is my story, man." Moses' face is now alive with excitement as the saga of his first inclusion with the Real Great Society begins. "I've been locked up. I've been trying to do this and that. I hear you people are looking for some kind of strong leadership to maintain this shit. Chino listened and said 'Okay. It so happens we have a new program and I'm gonna put you there. It pays $50.00 a week, okay?' And I became a general helper around the office at 69 Suffolk Street."

Moses found the rest of 1968 and the beginning of 1969 comforting. He was accepted by those with whom he worked. He was not timid about offering suggestions which were often accepted and implemented. The relationships between Chino, Angelo, and Moses grew with time and the addition of responsibilities. Moses was frequently asked to manage the office whenever Chino or Angelo were away on other business. Later on, when Chino could not fulfill a speaking engagement, Moses was his replacement. "One day I just got this notice," Moses proudly declares, "that there's a director's meeting and my name was on it. That meant I was in a decision-making situation."

Moses had become interested in the development of a Media workshop, an offshoot of the RGS activities. Working with Paul Settener, Moses assisted in the creation of photo workshops, art classes, poster-making, and other craft activities. His sense of fulfillment and achievement was extremely high. He felt he was being creative and appreciated. He later developed two comic book programs, finally actualized by the kids working in the workshop. These comic books became very popular throughout the Lower East Side.

Although away from the various power plays that existed over at the RGS new headquarters at 7th Street and Avenue A, Moses was kept informed through Chino, who visited the Media workshop periodically. When the conflict between Chino's group and the newer element working with RGS became quite apparent, Chino announced to Moses that he had been thinking of forming a new nucleus to continue the aims first envisioned by Chino and Angelo back in 1964. Moses sums up these events by saying, "It already did what we wanted it to do. It is the only Puerto Rican organization that is purely Puerto Rican in its decision-making and guidance from the street. Nobody ever had that kind of power before. We proved what we intended to do. That former street gang guys can take over a neighborhood and, if we're left alone, can make the structure work. People who came to study our structure were dumbfounded to discover that our structure was the basic capitalistic framework. The basics that made this country were the same in RGS. And that was the human spirit. It was always more valuable than the bureaucratic process."

The idea evolved that those Chino was interested in should partici-pate in one action that could weld their experiences and outlooks. Sometime earlier, Angelo had gone on an expedition organized by the Outward Bound survival school. He had had thirty days living on a remote Maine island, scaling nearly vertical cliffs, and manning an open boat in the rough seas. Angelo found this experience a totally absorbing and challenging one. It was decided that Chino, Angelo, Crespo, Roy, Sal, and Moses would join a medical expedition to Mexico organized by the Outward Bound group in Colorado.

The major premise of the newly formed group was to develop new concepts in housing and life style potentials. They had all become aware that poorly planned and developed city areas breed all the problems they had known and grown up with. Chino had remembered the time R. Buckminster Fuller had come to speak to RGS. He had been impressed by the vision of this old man. He hadn't really believed that anyone in the older white society could be that bold and outspo-ken about the needs and hopes for a better tomorrow.

Chino made contact with Bucky, requesting his assistance to guide this new group. Bucky readily accepted Chino's invitation. A series of conversations ensued. When the group of six were ready to leave on the Outward Bound trip, Bucky promised $1,600 to cover basic expenses. The money was late in arriving, causing Chino and Angelo to use the name and credit of RGS to gather their equip-ment and to rent a car for the trip to Colorado. The ongoing conflict between Chino and Angelo and the RGS bureaucracy became utterly strained due to these actions, although the money spent was to be refunded from Bucky's gift. Moses' attitude towards these incidents is very positive. He states, "We said we only did that because it's expedient. We needed the time that was allotted us."

Everything the six young men expected from the Outward Bound excursion was more than fulfilled. They shared a new solidarity and strength, both personal and collective. Moses found this experience a very binding one. His relationship with Angelo, spotty in the past, became extremely solid. Moses, who is very sensitive to the swaying power plays and factors of control, says "I found that between Angelo and myself there wasn't any power struggle in the psychological or physiological patterns. We were a team (including Crespo), and I cooked. I had a little more talent than the other guys for cooking, but once in a while Crespo would say, 'Hey, I want to cook tonight.' We were a unit separated from the rest of the expedition, basically because they were white."

Moses actively turned to the Media Workshop with new zeal and interest after this trip. The other members of CHARAS became involved with studies conducted by Michael Ben-Eli on geodesic principles. "CHARAS wasn't only on paper. We were struggling for funds at that time and I needed to do something in order to get some money. So I continued working for the Media Workshop. I then developed two comic book projects: *Blank Comics* and *Street Comics*."

Moses' need for physical activity led him to devote his time and attention to the Media Workshop and to relinquish his opportunity to join the classes established by Michael which he (Moses) found passive. "I don't like to sit around and do nothing," Moses says animatedly. "I mean, if something got to be done, bang, I go and we do it. But a lot of times at CHARAS we had to sit around and talk, or ask someone for something, and I don't particularly dig that. I'm tired of begging people." Moses then contributed his time and energy when it was directly needed. He allowed the ongoing activities to be conducted by the others in whom he had committed his trust and faith.

Moses now leans forward and speaks confidently as he says, "Well, the first thing I would need now to assume more responsibility in CHARAS is for them to get some bread for everybody. Outside of that mundane shit, I think CHARAS is a very powerful concept. Its power lies in the fact that it is the future."

Moses rises and begin pacing the room. An old feeling of enthusiasm and meaningfulness is evident in his voice and expression. "When I have talked to people who are poor in spirit, be they Spanish, black, or white, people who need to feel part of this world, and I tell them the story of CHARAS, their eyes light up. They say, goddamn that is something beautiful. And, maybe, they have been turned on to find their own resources to do something, somewhere."

169

Deep within Moses' heart, he is restless to return to the halcyon days of his early involvement with the Real Great Society and the Outward Bound expedition. He seems to crave the purity of existence he experienced then. The pressures of his current life occasionally obscure his vision. But it is apparent that the inner fire can be quickly ignited given the proper conditions. Moses would, it appears, gladly give up his present hustle and bustle. He wants to serve his people. He only has to be given the chance and he will again.

Sal Becker

"It's a strange feeling, you know. You wonder what makes a person have commitments after spending years and years doing nothing. The, all of a sudden something happens to you. I'm sure it happened with others involved in CHARAS. You just develop a whole set of values—a whole different value image. You wake up one morning and you see the whole world differently. You take the tools and the techniques that you've grown up with and you have to set other examples."

These incisive observations are made by a handsome, black-bearded, twenty-six-year-old young man who has learned to be truthful. Sal Becker doesn't bullshit himself. He doesn't try to bullshit the world around him either.

When he was ten years old, Sal had to learn a whole new set of life standards. His family only moved one block in the Lower East Side, but the entire perspective of his life had to change or he would not have survived.

His father owned a candy store at 14th Street and Avenue A. To his father, Sal was the center of the world. His father, an Italian, was proud of fathering a son who would carry on his tradition. Sal's mother had never married this man named Mesena, but that fact never disturbed the warmth and love that was Sal's for his first ten years. Sal's older brother and sister, his mother's children from a previous marriage, lived with him. There was another brother and sister that Sal hardly knew, who lived with his mother's divorced husband in upper New York state. Sal was his mother's fifth child. But in the Mesena household, Sal was number one.

The showering of attention and goodies came to an abrupt end when Sal's father died. They had lived next door to the 14th Street candy store. The sudden loss necessitated a move. An apartment was found on East 13th Street. What had been a predominantly Italian neighborhood for Sal's first ten years had now become totally Puerto Rican. New customs, attitudes, and experiences soon engulfed the pampered boy. Surrounded by a poverty he had never known, Sal had to become aware that the world did not revolve around his whims and needs.

Sal's mother, of German and Scottish extraction, was from Nova Scotia. Her first husband came from upstate New York German stock. Sal's father was Italian. The man that his mother married, two years after the death of Mr. Mesena, was Lithuanian. Thus, there was a "melting pot" atmosphere in Sal's life. But nothing prepared him for the onslaught of a Puerto Rican ghetto and hostile Italian neighbors.

Sal now works in a community youth workshop. He is married to an alert and knowing Puerto Rican girl, Helen, and they have a young son. As his father was proud of his son, Sal is of his. "But," he says, "I want my son to grow up in the city. I want him to grow up with kids that are poor and going through changes. I don't want him to have everything that he wants. Sure, I'll control his life somewhat, so that he doesn't get into any of the shit that I got into. But I want him to be an aware person. Not like the people I first grew up with, before moving to 13ᵗʰ Street."

Sal has very alienated feelings toward the Italians with whom he spent his first ten years. His eyes become steely when he talks about those days and people. "Listen, I want you to know that my father was full-blooded Italian. But the people at 14ᵗʰ and Avenue A were another breed. I try to envision myself growing up on Avenue A with the Italian kids that were there. I see them today. I'm just so happy I wasn't a victim of their sickness and prejudice. Their attitudes about people that don't think like them. Who don't do what they do. And it's amazing how they spend their days standing around guarding little corners of the block and just wasting time. I'd see the parents notice a black or Puerto Rican woman walking down the street. Right away they'd call her a whore or something. This was in front of the kids. The whole disrespect, for any kind of person but Italian, was amazing. There may be racism in every nationality but I developed a shield, a protective barrier against this kind of person. I'm just glad I moved away from those people."

Sal readily admits the young Puerto Ricans he encountered on East 13ᵗʰ Street were far more mature than he was. They had gone through changes that he, living a lower-middle class existence, had never imagined. "Everything was different. Their homes, their families, their relatives, the street. Man, the street particularly. The street, their poverty made them go through changes that grown-ups hadn't gone through. It was a shock and I had to adapt, and I had to fit in, mostly, because I wanted to. The next six years were some trip to me, let me tell you."

At sixteen, not liking school, Sal forged his birth certificate and enlisted in the Air Force. Two years later, Sal was back on the street after being bounced from the Air Force for being friendly with an airman involved in a base supply robbery. Falsely charged with the possession of grass, Sal successfully fought the accusation and was discharged with all the benefits due him.

The streets Sal came back to were different from those he had left. Drugs were now a common companion of street youth. He was introduced to speed and quickly got strung out. For one year he'd blow his mind. Then for two years he'd have odd jobs making $65 or $70 a week, just drifting, without direction or care.

The Real Great Society had become a vibrant force on the Lower East Side during Sal's aimless period. It was the Sanitation Department's strike in February, 1968 that prompted the start of the 13th Street block association. Sal was living with his mother at this time. He was persuaded to join the organization drive and the activities that followed. They helped clear the street of the accumulated garbage. Then a storefront office was opened. Soon, funding from the Community Lower East Side Corporation enabled them to start a summer program for the kids living on 13th Street between 1st and 2nd Avenues. Sal had now become addicted with the spirit of community participation and involvement.

By the summer of 1969, the funding ran out. RGS came to the rescue of the 13th Street block association by suggesting that the members become involved with a VISTA program. This program enlisted workers that had been previously busted on any kind of narcotics charge. Sal and many other members of the 13th Street group qualified. Sal became a VISTA worker from May to November. He organized support programs for the kids and community-action activities for the adult population on the block.

It was in August of 1969, while in VISTA, that Chino first sent Sal to the Outward Bound program. Sal, again in January, 1970, went with the newly formed CHARAS group to Mexico on another Outward Bound trip. Outward Bound is a tough survival fitness program. Chino had a plan for Sal, and the Outward Bound program was to be the first step. If Sal completed the work and tasks assigned to him while in Outward Bound, then, maybe Chino would approach Sal for participation in something else that was brewing in his mind.

During his first Outward Bound trip, for 26 days, Sal was put through vigorous physical and psychological self-testing. He was one of thirteen young men who were living on a Maine island totally on their own. For three days they were isolated and had to survive and return to home base. The most harrowing experience for Sal was climbing a 90-foot rock cliff with only a rope linking him to another person. It was not only the responsibility of someone else's life that frightened Sal, but the fact he didn't know how to swim. It was the fall to into the ocean waters below that terrified Sal. As he retells these experiences, he breathes a little faster. Sal releases a heavy sigh of relief when he completes telling this incident. He looks at you with renewed awareness of his strengths and weaknesses. "Okay," he says, "I was 21 at the time, but I grew up fast from those 26 days of tough living."

The RGS group decided they wanted as many Lower East Siders as possible to know the rigors of an Outward Bound experience. They realized that if you could survive the physical and mental stress, then any other form of stress could be easier to absorb and cope with. Various attempts at securing an RGS operation in Outward Bound did not materialize. But toward the end of 1969, contact was made with a Colorado Outward Bound unit that was going into Mexico. They were to establish a medical expedition to inoculate Mexican Indians against measles, smallpox, and tetanus. The future members of CHARAS went on this trip.

By the time Sal returned to New York, in February of 1970, Chino was ready to confront him. An encounter session was held with various people who were soon to form CHARAS. Everything was laid open during this meeting. Everyone was ripped into. No one was spared. Whatever reservations of questions one had about another were aired and talked out. Finally, Angelo turned to Sal and demanded, "Look, do you still want to work with us or stay with VISTA?" Sal thought deeply for a split moment and shot back, "Both, you mother fucker. You knew you'd get me involved. So what do you want me to do?" Angelo and Chino sat back and laughed. Everyone else laughed and embraced one another in true understanding and affection. Sal was now the 'S' of the soon-to-be-organized CHARAS.

Both Chino and Angelo had, through Fred Good, made contact with Bucky Fuller sometime earlier. Bucky had been invited to talk at an RGS meeting in 1968, and they had listened carefully. They began to think of what was said and decided they wanted active involvement in attempting solutions to low-income housing problems. The geodesic dome idea fascinated them. Although they knew nothing of the mathematics needed, they were undeterred and felt they could overcome any obstacle with direct effort and strong commitment. Chino and Angelo believed they needed Sal's tenacity of purpose and sense of devotion to round out their new group. Most assuredly, Sal was able to contribute these qualities.

Soon, Michael Ben-Eli was teaching them algebra at the 13th street storefront block-association space. Sal remembers the difficulty he had. He also remembers how much easier it was for Roy. Roy had previous training and experience with IBM. Few of the others had had any successful background in mathematics. But they persevered.

By July, 1970, Sal and Helen were married. He now became concerned with supporting his new wife. A job with the Neighborhood Youth Corps was the answer. Sal helped establish a photo workshop for the youth of the Lower East Side. He also continued his association with CHARAS by tracking special research projects or helping in the fund-raising drives that went on all the time.

"He was this almighty, important figure that came from never-never land to the Lower East Side." Sal was remembering the first time he saw Bucky in the middle of May, 1970. Bucky had come to the loft on Cherry Street. Everyone was excited that Bucky was to see what they were planning. Sal, particularly, wanted to meet Bucky. He knew that Angelo and Chino had developed a warm relationship with him. That afternoon, Chino had gone around introducing "Brother Bucky" to everyone. Bucky looked pleased at being called "brother."

Sal recaptures the drama and electric sensation of the occasion as he says, "For a small man, he's very dynamic. I almost felt energy coming off him. It radiated when he walked around. Man, I wanted the experience of talking to him so I could tell my grandchildren, tell other people." Sal didn't get the chance he wanted. He did, however, see Bucky relating to his friends with an interest and concern that overwhelmed him. "Bucky would put a hand to his ear and listen to you." Sal's eyes radiate as he recalls that memorable event. "I could see he really liked Chino, Angelo, and Roy. He always wanted to do things for them. Well, you know how Chino is. He's here, but he's not. He's always thinking of something to organize. And Bucky would see this and pull him back and say, 'Did you hear me? Did you understand what I said?' and Chino would say 'Yeah' and go on introducing Bucky as 'Brother Bucky.' It was nice."

Bucky's involvement with CHARAS is a fantastic wonderment to Sal. Considering Bucky as one of the world's greatest men, Sal is continually amazed at Bucky's concern and interest in the kind of guys he grew up with and learned to love. But he recognizes the deep core of humanity in Bucky. "He's a humble man, you know. He's kind, and he wanted you to understand that, too. He didn't want you to think he would just turn you off because you were less important than he was. He'd put himself on your level. And it worked. To Chino, Angelo, and all the rest of us, Bucky's a household name now. We've become so attached. It's a beautiful relationship."

Although Sal is not now actively involved with the daily activities of CHARAS, his concern has not diminished. The bonds of friendship and shared experiences are too strong. Sal communicated this ongoing concern and appreciation when he says, "I can tell you for a fact, all of us have developed such a relationship that we could throw fire at each other and still keep the friendship. We can do that because we know that we have made a commitment to each other. We care about each other. There's no selfishness involved with each other. It's a beautiful thing. We really love each other. I wouldn't change it for the world. I want you to know I get along better with other people because of them. It's fantastic."

Sal doesn't say it, but he surely hopes to be able to pass these feelings on to his son. Sal wants his son to be a spiritual member of CHARAS. That's if he can cut it.

Conclusion

The people of CHARAS may occasionally attempt to outreach their actual potential. But the reaching is strengthening. In the past they may have boasted of more than they accomplished. Nevertheless, they give others the hope and vision that change is possible. To people of the ghetto who live an existence with few alternatives, CHARAS has shown that life need not be a series of dead ends.

There is the enthusiasm of an emerging new nation in the activities and aspirations of CHARAS. There is the fierce pride of wanting giant accomplishments and the resentment that the establishment is not always in concert with them. But an active understanding and knowledge of how to cope with these forces is developing and expanding.

Coming out of a basic street condition, the patterns of "jiving the man" are still very much part of their working mechanism. There is still healthy distrust of the society. And the distrust is justifiable. They have also become the creators and victims of myth-making. In the "street" you must pretend more than exists. Great damage can be perpetrated, though, if this practice is constant and unabating.

Fortunately, the lessons of the past seem to deter the workers at CHARAS from acts of self-delusion or excessive exaggeration. Their activities seemed rooted to the community and the needs expressed by what they have experienced.

It is the extension of hope that is CHARAS' greatest asset. As long as the on-going participants of CHARAS sustain this tenuous possibility, then they will have an important contribution to make to their immediate community and the other situations they may affect. It is fervently expected that this attitude will continue and expand. The courage shown by CHARAS must be expanded and other groups need to be similarly stimulated and structured. A network of groups like CHARAS can turn the tide of negativism in ghetto life. Acts of self-realization and fulfillment can be the result for many who have given up all attempts at effecting any change in their lives. It takes time and great effort. But it can be done. It is important to remember in this instance that the process is more important than the product.

It would be sad if the towel was thrown in just as round one begins.

Interview
Michael Ben-Eli
& Ben Estes

Michael Ben-Eli standing with the 1973 edition, near the original dome building site. April 21, 2017. Photographed by Ben Estes.

After his mentorship work with CHARAS, Michael Ben-Eli went on to establish the Sustainability Lab, an initiative that engages in research, development, and education activities focused around key sustainability-related issues. Ben Estes, the founder of The Song Cave, sat down with Michael Ben-Eli at Situations Gallery (located steps from the original dome building site) on April 21st, 2017 for this interview.

◆ Ben Estes: Michael, hello, thank you for sitting with me today to talk about *CHARAS, The Improbable Dome Builders*, your involvement with the group, and a bit about what has happened since the publication of the book in 1973. Unfortunately, Chino was unable to join us today, his voice and memories will certainly be missed here this afternoon.

I guess a place for us to begin would be where the book finishes: the dome has been built, Fuller has arrived onsite, and then…

◆ Michael Ben-Eli: The dome was destroyed! Well, you know, we had built it on that lot without permits, illegally, so to speak. We had another dome, a very nice one, a smaller one, that we built a little later, on the site of the old brewery, on 93rd street? But both were taken down. And as you know, the CHARAS group started doing work here in the Lower East Side. They've been here for a long time.

◆ B: What kind of projects were they involved in?

◆ M: It's no longer the case, but at the time there were a lot of abandoned buildings down here, where landlords couldn't pay the taxes or whatever the case was, and CHARAS started renovating some of those old buildings to help homeless people in this area and develop access to housing with them. We ourselves were actually squatting in one of those deserted buildings while we were working on the dome. As you can see in many of the pictures in the book, the office where Roy was working and where he lived was in such a space. Later, the city gave the group a large building, an old school near Tompkins Square Park, Avenue C, I think, where they were able to set up a cultural center, including an art gallery, where they showed movies and hosted talks and meetings. It was a very active place. Now, I'm not sure of the specifics, but there are some issues of tearing the building down. It is too bad that Chino is not with us today, because I am not familiar with the exact details. I think that when the city gave them the right to use this building, there were some limits placed on future development possibilities there, and that's what they're trying to use now as leverage, so they can stay in the building and continue with their many important community programs. Meanwhile, all activities there have had to cease.

● B: The idea of public housing in relation to dome building comes up a number of times in the book, and hearing about CHARAS' later work in renovating abandoned buildings for the homeless.

● M: The project wasn't really ever about creating public housing. Their whole plan, originally, was to get out, to leave New York City. During those years, in the late 60s and early 70s—this was just after Woodstock—people were setting up communes all over the country, drop-out cities I think they were called. Using domes became very popular and, in fact, domes kind of became a symbol of the counter-culture. When the group was first introduced to Fuller, their idea was to leave the city and set up such a commune.

● B: Right, didn't Fuller even give them a plot of land?

● M: Yes! Fuller's idea was that he'd give them a piece of land that he owned near Woodstock, Vermont, and that he'd send me over here to quickly teach them how to build a dome, and then they'd go up there and build their own domes, and live happily ever after. I came to New York for a couple of weeks, but as we know it ended up being a lot longer!

They intuitively felt that it was important for them to get out of the city. Again, it was a very

different environment here in those years, rife with drugs and crime, and many of them already had a history that had put them in prison, including some serious stuff. So, they thought that if they were able to get away from the heart of the city, they'd be in better shape.

● B: But they never left...

● M: They actually stayed and ended up doing very important work within the city itself. It was kind of an unusual, spontaneous effort of the counter-culture at the time to organize within the city. I think that a similar need exists even now. There is so much controversy, on the west side, in Chelsea, for example, where developers are putting pressure on a community that was fairly quiet and stable for a long time, where working class people had lived for ages and now that land values have skyrocketed and developers are forcing people out, citizen groups are forming and organizing themselves. I think that CHARAS was an early version of this kind of local communities getting together.

● B: You mean you see this as a modern-day version of the utopic, counter-culture ideas that you were speaking about earlier?

● M: It doesn't need to be regarded as utopian, it's a very practical matter. You have to live in a place, and you have to try to create conditions for a better life.

And as I see it, CHARAS was successful in doing that—by creating their community center, all of the public programming, the activities for kids—really carving out a place for themselves within their urban context and trying to make it a better place.

◆ B: But in some ways that *is* utopic, isn't it?

◆ M: The reason that I'm trying to get away from that term is because "utopia" indicates a dream, or something unreal—and I'm saying that there are practical day-to-day issues that don't need a brand-new reality in order to be addressed. So, to the extent that individuals and groups take the initiative themselves, and don't wait for the government, and don't wait for others to do it for them, they can bring about effective, positive change. Individuals and groups can take the initiative and seek out what is needed to better one's own life, and that's what members of CHARAS were doing. It's actually a very practical issue.

◆ B: Did your experience with these "practical ideas" being used for larger results have any effect on your own future philosophies toward teaching, or your development of The Sustainability Lab?

◆ M: In retrospect it obviously has a lot to do with what I have going on now. For the connection, however, we need to take a step back. I was originally made aware of the kinds of issues that today fall under the "sustainability" umbrella when I first met Fuller as a young student of Architecture in London. The term "sustainability" didn't exist in those days. Fuller was dealing with questions about the world's resources and our relationship to the environment already then, in the early sixties. Fuller, addressing the architectural world, was talking about the whole planet as an object of design. To me, architecture had meant Frank Lloyd Wright, or Le Corbusier. I'd never thought in these kinds of bigger terms before. The encounter with him opened my eyes to these ideas and I began working with him, and became more and more interested in these issues—which I increasingly saw as issues of management. It implied the management of the world's resources and the way we interact with each other and with the world. I got very interested in the system-sciences, especially cybernetics, sensing that in these disciplines a new epistemology was being developed to deal with complexity. What is the nature of complex systems? How do they adapt and evolve? How do they organize themselves?

In England, there was work being done, notably by Stafford Beer, who was importing concepts of cybernetics to addressing management issues. Looking at organizations as organisms, and looking at how their internal structures related to the ways they function, and dealing with questions of change. I gravitated to this work and became interested in questions concerning change management, since major change is what we need to bring about in the world today. Beyond the dome itself, CHARAS was a great opportunity to experiment, informally, with facilitating change at a community level.

⬢ B: In reading the book, it felt to me that many members of CHARAS had possibly missed that internal structure and feeling of community that they had had while they were active gang members, and had felt it necessary then to organize themselves in a new way. The organizational elements of gang life, the rules that they lived by, hadn't worked well for them. Before, the community of their gang was the main organizing factor of their lives, and it's interesting to think about that through the lens of the sciences that you're talking about…

⬢ M: Of course, because it's a question that is completely significant both on a local scale, like those local urban groups of citizens, and also on a global scale where humanity *has* to organize itself in a different way. That's the impetus that started this project for them. When Fuller asked me to come and work with

them, I was interested in experimenting with the use of paperboard and ferro-cement in developing light, simple shelter structures, and the CHARAS request presented an opportunity to pursue that, clearly, in an unusual context. The connection then, that I can only see now in retrospect, is that the kinds of projects that we're trying to initiate and develop at The Lab are projects that are unconventional, that look impossible, and yet succeed outside of the realm of common institutional conventions. The CHARAS project was obviously of this kind. It resonated with something that I'd reacted to instinctively. I mean, there was no money, no stable working environment, I came to New York and didn't have a place to live at first. I took on that challenge although it was not a challenge that made sense in a professional or career-building type of way. And I find myself now, with the Sustainability Lab's flagship project with the Bedouins in the Negev Desert, that it's actually, in many ways, CHARAS revisited, on a much larger scale.

⬢ B: Which brings me to a question I'm very interested in hearing your answer to—what you think a project like CHARAS would have to look like today?

⬢ M: Well, I think if I were to do a project like this now, in an urban environment—remember, in the case of CHARAS the project involved mainly two aspects: helping the group to organize and do something, so there is a community aspect, and then there was an object, a structure, a piece of simple technology: a prototype dome which had no chance of surviving long where it was built.

So today, it would not be just a dome. I don't think domes, at this scale, make sense in an urban setting in terms of effective land and space use. Unless it's a much bigger dome, that can cover huge areas. So today, I would approach it differently and much more comprehensively in the sense that I would use the set of sustainability principles that we've developed at The Lab, to set the frame for the project. That would mean you'd want to integrate the community, the people who live there, the question of economic viability: Is it self-sufficient? How does it relate to an economically productive activity of some sort? Maybe it should include urban food production of some sort. You'd certainly want it connected to an infrastructure of green technologies: energy, water, waste, recycling. I think the whole question of who owns what and how decisions are made, the underlying governance structure of this hypothetical urban setting, all of these would be included. I think it could be a fascinating thing to do.

◆ B: Do you think there is a possibility that you may get involved in another project like this, here?

◆ M: Well, you know, one of the ideas behind The Lab is to set up a network of research, development, and education centers around the world that are mapped onto particular eco-zones. I believe that thinking in land use management terms provides a much more helpful conceptual framework to use than prevailing distinctions such as North and South, developed and under-developed, poor and rich, and the like. A desert is a desert regardless of whether it is in Arizona, China, or in the Middle East. So we'd like to set up a network of such eco-zone centers, and we've already started with two. One in Israel, in the Negev desert, dealing with dryland issues, and another in Costa Rica for dry and humid tropical zones. We'd like to expand that, so we're talking about something possibly in the Galapagos dealing with island ecology, maybe in Bhutan for alpine ecology, and I'd like very much to do something in New York City, to set up a center for urban ecology. I think this would be a great place for it, it'd be very exciting.

◆ B: There's definitely a need.

◆ M: There certainly is one.

◆ B: What are your feelings towards local movements like Occupy Wall Street?

◆ M: I think the problem with something like Occupy Wall Street is that these are popular one-time events. They don't have enough of an operational focus, and in the end are not very productive. They just dissipate. I think over time, if such events persist, they can be useful for changing public mood. But they are not organized as a design initiative. They are not really organized to design and produce a new way of doing things, a lasting change. Remember, Bucky has this beautiful quote "If you want to change something don't fight it, just create a new model." Occupying Wall Street does not create a new model. They said "we don't like" something, but they did not articulate clearly what they do like, what a desired end-state would be, or how to go about it. That element is totally missing from those phenomena, instead they are simply pointing out a negative. Which is important for awareness, but not enough if actual, effective change is desired.

◆ B: If there was something that you'd hope readers could take away from this book, what would you hope for it to be?

◆ M: Well, I think first would be that there are opportunities to do a lot of positive things! Things that might not be immediately self-evident. And I think young people in particular should seek those kinds of opportunities, and

not simply follow convention. I can see change in this regard as well. At The Lab, we set up a very interesting graduate program called the Global Sustainability Fellows program, to address the need to produce stronger leaders in the future, leaders with better and deeper understanding of sustainability issues. The program is set up for students from all over the world, and the idea is that while they pursue their degrees in their chosen field— architecture, urban planning, law, health, art, you name it—those who want to get deeper exposure to the ideas and tools that are required for the transition that has to be designed deliberately, the model of the future if you like, would come for two summer sessions—one summer focused on concepts, the second summer on actual work. We did the first round in Costa Rica, and the outcome was work we did with a local community of stateless Nicaraguan refugees who'd moved to Costa Rica and stayed there. A desperately poor community. They have nothing. So, we worked with the community to come up with a concept for a long-term project that could change their living conditions. The plan is to address legal and tenure issues, education and job creation, the infrastructure, housing, health, all of these things. The world-wide refugee crisis in only growing and such a project could be a model for a sensible way of dealing with migrant communities in Costa Rica and elsewhere.

I'm telling this long story because I could see in many of the students that we attracted, young people that are deeply concerned about the state of the world, and unsatisfied with what academia or the "normal" professions could offer them. They are as bright and accomplished as any. They could go work on Wall Street, they could go anywhere, but they say "this is not what I want to do." Instead they are looking for opportunities to participate in bringing about meaningful change. Some of the students have been working with us since, and we're looking to launch a new project, called Project Transition, with that community in Costa Rica, where we can create more opportunities for people who want to participate in radical innovation.

⬡ B: And this book does offer a portrait of radical innovators...

⬡ M: Absolutely, it was a very exciting time. Members of the CHARAS group took on something that looked impossible and demonstrated what they could do with it. One idea that I got from this, that has stayed with me over the years, is to use projects not only for their end result, in this case a prototype dome, but to create a working, development process that is an educational process as well: technically, skill-wise, but emotionally and spiritually as well. You don't just deliver an object. If you can get the community involved on that level, everyone taking part will be transformed.

Finally, as we close, I want to pay a special tribute to Syeus, who wrote the book. Syeus was an inspired photographer and theater director and producer, who was deeply sensitive to the social and economic issues of the time. He was a great friend, and I often miss him.

Technical Description
Michael Ben-Eli

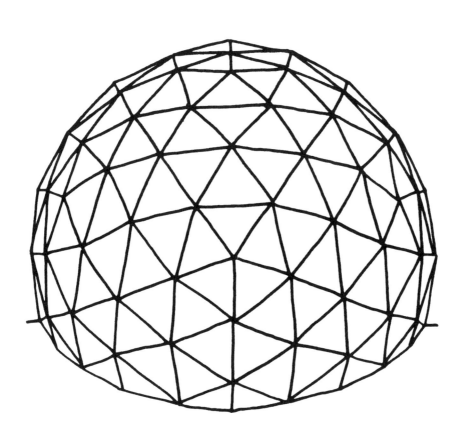

Following is a basic description of Fuller's Geodesic Geometry, and the technical details of the CHARAS dome.

⬢ 1. GENERAL DESCRIPTION

Geodesic domes were invented and first developed by R. Buckminster Fuller. Their geometry is usually derived from two geometric solids for reasons of economy and structural integrity. The first is the icosahedron, a solid with 20 equal triangular faces; the second is the so called triacontahedron which can be derived from the icosahedron and has 30 equal diamonds as faces.

ILLUSTRATION A

Icosahedron
General View

The triacontahedron can be derived by joining mid-points on the surface of the icosahedron.

ILLUSTRATION B1

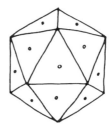

Mid-points on surface of icosahedron.

ILLUSTRATION B2

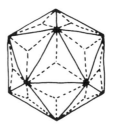

Joining mid-points to obtain edges of triacontahedron.

ILLUSTRATION B3

The Triacontahedron—A Solid With 30 Equal Diamond Faces.

To understand how the geometry of the icosahedron, for instance, relates to a sphere, imagine "exploding," or blowing up this solid to the surface of a sphere: the result will be a spherical icosahedron.

ILLUSTRATION C

The Spherical Icosahedron

Here we have a network of 20 equilateral spherical triangles. The maximum possible on a surface of a sphere.

Depending on the diameter of a specific dome to be constructed, the material used and the type of elements, i.e., linear members or surface triangles, each one of the basic 20 icosahedron triangles will be further subdivided. We shall obtain a typical "geodesic" pattern.

ILLUSTRATION D

A Typical Geodesic Pattern

This subdivision is usually called frequency and relates to the subdivision of the faces of the basic icosahedron triangle (one of the 20), hence we get:

ILLUSTRATION E

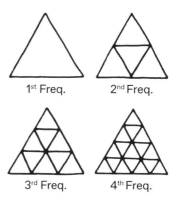

1st Freq.   2nd Freq.

3rd Freq.   4th Freq.

Frequency Subdivisions of Basic Icosahedron Triangles

Other types of subdivisions exist but this is a very common one and should serve to get the idea across.

What is usually done in design and computation of a geodesic structure is briefly the following:

1. You take one spherical icosahedron triangle (one is enough as all 20 are equilateral and symmetrically distributed on the surface of a sphere).
2. You decide on the frequency subdivision to be used according to circumstances.
3. You compute the arches corresponding to the edges of spherical triangles, (using principles of spherical trigonometry).
4. You derive the chords, respective to these arches with which one can get the final dimensions of relevant length of members or sides of panels.

ILLUSTRATION F1

Spherical Icosa

ILLUSTRATION F2

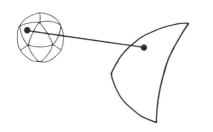

An Isolated Basic
Spherical Triangle

ILLUSTRATION F3

Basic Spherical Triangle And
2nd Frequency Subdivision

ILLUSTRATION F4

Desired Chords Corresponding
to Arches Obtained by 2nd
Frequency Subdivision.

Obviously, the higher the frequency, the more 'spherical' the final structure. Ideal spherocity, however, is usually not the most critical objective and the frequency subdivision will be decided upon according to the diameter of the structure and the ideal size of elements in terms of strength and convenient handling.

Everything that has been said thus far about the icosahedron is relevant to the triacontahedron geometry as well. In the later case, we relate to a basic triacontahedron diamond rather than the basic icosahedron triangle. For different frequencies we shall get (again one typical possibility):

ILLUSTRATION G1

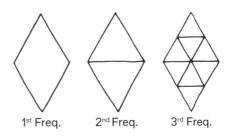

1st Freq.   2nd Freq.   3rd Freq.

Frequency Subdivisions of
Triacontahedron Diamond

A good reason to use the triacontahedron geometry is that usually, for a given frequency, it will allow the use of a smaller number of different triangles with resulting higher simplicity and better economy.

◆ 2. GEOMETRY

In the case of the CHARAS dome, the four frequency triacontahedron subdivision was used. Here each basic diamond was subdivided as follows:

ILLUSTRATION H

4 Frequency Triacontahedron
—Typical Diamond

To ease the identification of triangles and mapping their positions, a code system is used in which each tip of every triangle (or the points of intersections in the triangular network), is given a letter name. Here to it is enough to deal with only one typical diamond as the pattern will repeat itself throughout the structure.

ILLUSTRATION I

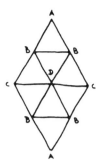

Basic diamond and
code system used.

In each one of these diamonds, we have 8 triangles in two different pairs of four (in each pair of four the triangles are equal to each other).

ILLUSTRATION J

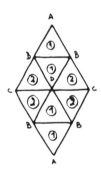

4 triangles numbered (1) are
equal to each other.

4 triangles numbered (2) are
equal to each other.

In other words, our whole dome can be constructed with only two different triangular elements.

ILLUSTRATION K

One is triangle CBD.
And the other is triangle ABB,
which is equal to triangle DBB.

ILLUSTRATION L

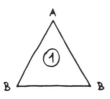

A typical view showing coding
system and distribution of triangles in the structure is the
following mapping, which is used
to identify positions of triangles
during construction.

ILLUSTRATION M

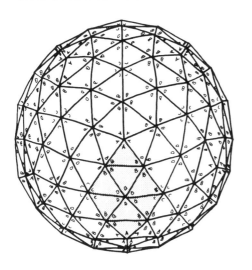

4 Frequency Triacontahedron
—A Typical View

● 3. STRUCTURE & CONSTRUCTION

The CHARAS dome was built
using triangular elements cut
from special paperboard tested
to compressive loads of 1000 lbs.
sq. inch. Each triangular element
has folding flaps which when
folded inwardly (towards center
of the dome) produce a stiff triangular box. Such boxes are then
assembled and bolted together
following the mapping system.

ILLUSTRATION N

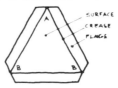

A Typical Paper-Board Triangle

ILLUSTRATION O

A Typical Stiff Triangular Box

Certain sections are left out
for desired openings. To offset
the structural effects of omit-
ting triangles, simple wooden
frames were introduced. A
wooden base anchored the
structure to the ground.
   With the same two basic
triangular elements, either a
hemisphere or a three-quarter
sphere can be built.

(A) A HEMISPHERE
4 Frequency Triacon Geodesic

Diameter	D=20'
Radius	R=10'
Floor Area	A=314 sq. ft.
Surface Area	S=628 sq. ft.

ILLUSTRATION P

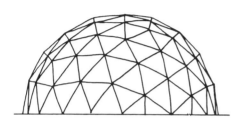

4 freq. triacon–½ sphere
(partial coding).

A ½ sphere consists of: 13 whole
diamonds with 8 triangles each:

ILLUSTRATION Q

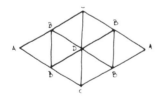

2 halve diamonds with
4 triangles each:

ILLUSTRATION R

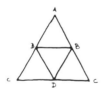

2 halve diamonds of
6 triangles each:

ILLUSTRATION S

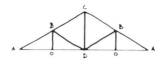

In the later case triangles
ABB & DBB are cut into two
halves as shown:

ILLUSTRATION T

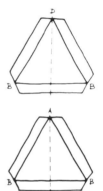

This means that for each
hemisphere we need:

NO. 1

Triangle (ABB)	32 pieces
Triangle (DBB)	32 pieces
Total	64 pieces

NO. 2

Triangle (BCD)	60

Total for each ½ sphere
124 triangles

(B) ¾ SPHERE
4 Frequency Triacon Geodesic

Diameter	D=20'
Radius	R=10'
Floor Area	A=250 sq. ft.
Surface Area	S=942 sq. ft.

ILLUSTRATION U

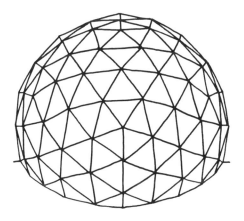

4 freq. triacon–¾ sphere
(partial coding)

(Notice truncation of all triangles above base level.)

The ¾ sphere consists of:
20 whole diamonds with 8 triangles each:

ILLUSTRATION V

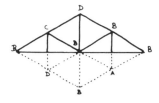

5 of the following configurations of 6 triangles each:

ILLUSTRATION W

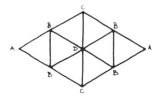

(Truncation here does not cut triangles exactly by two but is made to given measurements.)

For all intents and purposes, for each ¾ sphere we shall need:

NO. 1

Triangle (ABB)	50 pieces
Triangle (DBB)	50 pieces
Total	100 pieces

NO. 2

Triangle (BCD)	100

Total for each ¾ sphere
200 triangles

Various methods of coating can be used to give the paperboard structure a variety of length of 'life.' In the CHARAS dome, the paperboard shell was used as a form over which ½" ferro-cement shell was laid (see photographic illustrations). After the cement was cured the paperboard structure cold be retrieved to be used again or left in for its insulation value.

Image Dossier

200

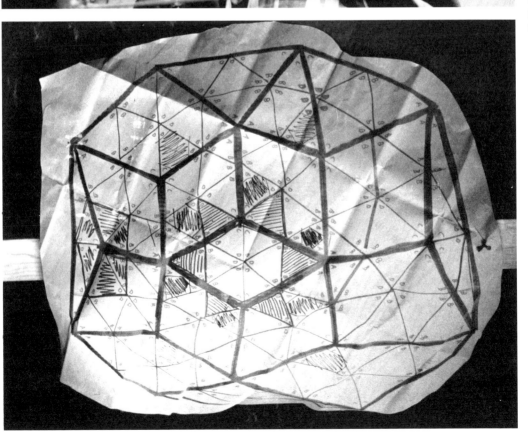

Above: Mark and Roy scoring the paper board sections.

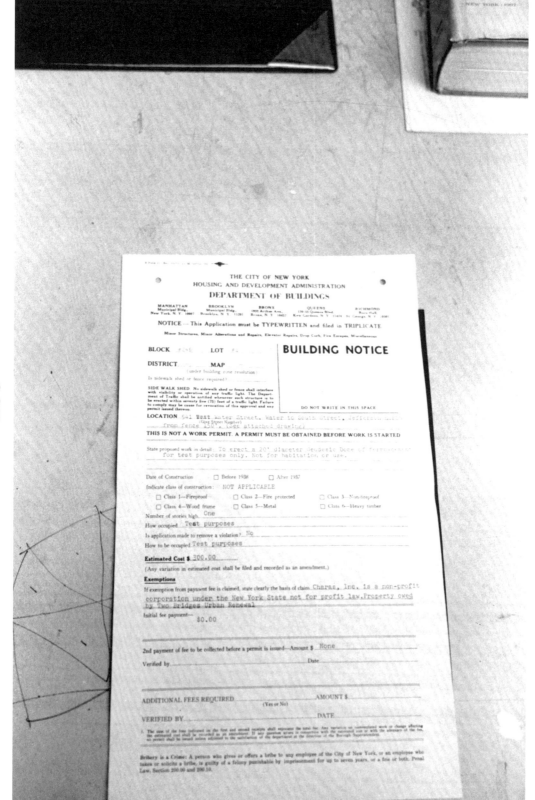

THE CITY OF NEW YORK
HOUSING AND DEVELOPMENT ADMINISTRATION
DEPARTMENT OF BUILDINGS

MANHATTAN	BROOKLYN	BRONX	QUEENS	RICHMOND
Municipal Bldg.	Municipal Bldg.	1932 Arthur Ave.	120-55 Queens Blvd.	Boro Hall
New York, N.Y. 10007	Brooklyn, N.Y. 11201	Bronx, N.Y. 10457	Kew Gardens, N.Y. 11424	St. George, N.Y. 10301

NOTICE — This Application must be TYPEWRITTEN and filed in TRIPLICATE

Minor Structures, Minor Alterations and Repairs, Elevator Repairs, Drop Curb, Fire Escapes, Miscellaneous

BLOCK ____ LOT ____

DISTRICT ____ MAP ____
(under building zone resolution)

Is sidewalk shed or fence required? ____

SIDE WALK SHED No sidewalk shed or fence shall interfere with visibility or operation of any traffic light. The Department of Traffic shall be notified whenever such structure is to be erected within seventy five (75) feet of a traffic light. Failure to comply may be cause for revocation of this approval and any permit issued thereon.

LOCATION 541 West Water Street, Water to South street, Jefferson Park
from fence 125' (see attached drawing)
(Give Street Number)

THIS IS NOT A WORK PERMIT. A PERMIT MUST BE OBTAINED BEFORE WORK IS STARTED

State proposed work in detail: To erect a 20' diameter Geodesic Dome of ferro-cement
for test purposes only. Not for habitation, or use.

Date of Construction ☐ Before 1938 ☐ After 1937

Indicate class of construction: NOT APPLICABLE

☐ Class 1—Fireproof   ☐ Class 2—Fire protected   ☐ Class 3—Non-fireproof
☐ Class 4—Wood frame   ☐ Class 5—Metal   ☐ Class 6—Heavy timber

Number of stories high. One

How occupied Test purposes

Is application made to remove a violation? No

How to be occupied Test purposes

Estimated Cost $ 700.00

(Any variation in estimated cost shall be filed and recorded as an amendment.)

Exemptions

If exemption from payment fee is claimed, state clearly the basis of claim. Charas, Inc. is a non-profit
corporation under the New York State not for profit law. Property owed
by Two Bridges Urban Renewal

Initial fee payment— $0.00

2nd payment of fee to be collected before a permit is issued—Amount $ None

Verified by ____ Date ____

ADDITIONAL FEES REQUIRED ____ AMOUNT $ ____
(Yes or No)

VERIFIED BY ____ DATE ____

3. The sum of the fees indicated in the first and second receipts shall represent the total fee. Any variation in contemplated work or change affecting the estimated cost shall be recorded as an amendment. If any question arises in connection with the estimated cost or with the adequacy of the fee, no permit shall be issued unless adjusted to the satisfaction of the department at the direction of the Borough Superintendent.

Bribery is a Crime: A person who gives or offers a bribe to any employee of the City of New York, or an employee who takes or solicits a bribe, is guilty of a felony punishable by imprisonment for up to seven years, or a fine or both. Penal Law, Section 200.00 and 200.10.

BUILDING NOTICE

DO NOT WRITE IN THIS SPACE

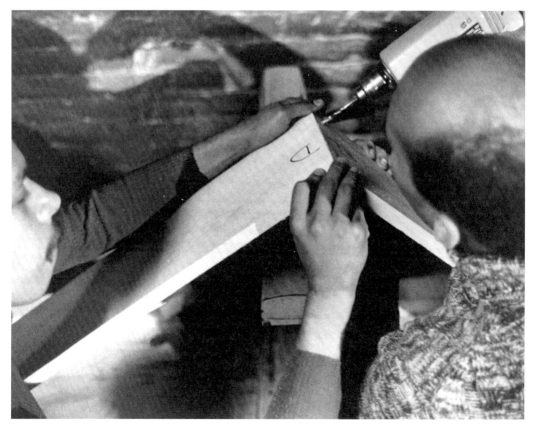

Below: Commissioner Joseph Stein and assistant John Harvell discuss the need for filing necessary papers with the Dept. of Buildings as Michael listens attentively.

211

Below: Sylvester John Perrone, a construction superintendent living in the neighborhood, offers advice to Michael.

Above: Fairfield Hoban, of World Magazine, assists the transport of diamond sections to the building site.

221

Final placement of paper board sections.

A stray dog became the dome's first tenant. Roy and James discuss this problem with the neighborhood kids who were caring for the dog.

228

Left: Sheeting is being cut to tautly shape around the dome frame. Right: Plastic sheeting is stapled to the wooden foundation blocks to protect the cardboard from water damage.

Securing plastic covering to the dome's surface.

233

Ferro-cement being mixed for application to dome's chicken wired surface.

Below: Local Firemen intrigued with the interior of a newly completed dome shell.

235

Syeus Mottel (1930–2014), a lifelong New Yorker, was a theater director and photographer noted for his documentation of Lee Strasberg at the Actors Studio, R. Buckminster Fuller, and the significant political and cultural figures of his time.

In 1965, Strasberg granted him exclusive permission to photograph the closed-door studio sessions of the Actors Studio, resulting in a ten-year photographic archive (1965–1975). Mottel then became Media Consultant to R. Buckminster Fuller, and widely published his documentation of Fuller's activities. He was also the credited photographer for the 1968 film *Symbiopsychotaxiplasm* directed by William Greaves.

Richard Buckminster "Bucky" Fuller (1895–1983) was an American architect, systems theorist, author, designer, and inventor. Fuller published more than 30 books, coining or popularizing terms such as "Spaceship Earth," "Ephemeralization," and "Synergetic." He also developed numerous inventions, mainly architectural designs, and popularized the widely known geodesic dome.

238

CHARAS
The Improbable Dome Builders

© 1973, 2017 Syeus Mottel
Pioneer Works Press
& The Song Cave

"Everybody's Business"
Courtesy, The Estate of
R. Buckminster Fuller.
All rights reserved.

Edition: 2000
ISBN: 978-1-945711-05-3
Printed in Belgium by Die Keure
Typeface: Favorit
Paper: 120 gsm Multioffset
Cover: 300 gsm Invercote G
Jacket: 120 gsm Multioffset

Editors: Ben Estes,
    Alan Felsenthal, Zach White
Assistant Editor: Katie Giritlian
Design: Daniel Kent

Distributed by
ARTBOOK | D.A.P.
75 Broad St., Suite 630
New York, NY 10004
artbook.com

This book is circulated in partnership
with the D.U.C. Library Program of Art
Resources Transfer. The D.U.C. places
free contemporary art books in public
schools and libraries nationwide. Visit
artresourcestransfer.org to learn more.

○
▢▢▢
Pioneer Works Press
159 Pioneer St., Brooklyn, NY 11231
pioneerworks.org

The Song Cave
56 4th Place, Brooklyn, NY 11231
the-song-cave.com

The Song Cave is dedicated to recovering
a lost sensibility and creating a new one
by publishing books of poetry, translations,
art criticism, and making art prints and
other related materials.

Pioneer Works is a cultural center dedicated to experimentation, education and
production across disciplines. Through
a broad range of educational programs,
performances, residencies and exhibitions,
Pioneer Works transcends disciplinary
boundaries to foster a community where
alternative modes of thought are activated
and supported. We strive to make culture
available to all. Pioneer Works is a non-
profit 501(c)(3).

Pioneer Works programs are made
possible by the generous support of our
board of directors, grants, and donations.

239